Julia López-Robe

Celebrating Our Cuentos

Choosing and Using Latinx Literature in Elementary Classrooms

DEDICACIÓN

A la memoria de mis padres, Lázaro y Ana Rosa López,
quienes me siguen inspirando

Publisher/Content editor: Lois Bridges
Editorial director: Sarah Longhi
Editor-in-chief/Development editor: Raymond Coutu
Senior editor: Shelley Griffin
Production editor: Danny Miller
Designer: Maria Lilja
Content reviewers: Jerusha Saldaña Yañez and Alexandra Gomez

Photos ©: cover: Illustrations made by Carloz Velez Aguiler/Astound Us for Scholastic Inc.; 16: spass/Shutterstock; 19: Aliaksei Tarasau/Shutterstock; 28: SDI Productions/Getty Images; 31: Monkey Business Images/Shutterstock; 47: Ababsolutum/Getty Images; 113: SDI Productions/Getty Images; 129: SDI Productions/Getty Images. All other photos courtesy of the author.

2 3 4 5 6 7 8 9 10   40   30 29 28 27 26 25 24 23 22 21

Scholastic Inc., 557 Broadway, New York, NY 10012

Contents

ACKNOWLEDGMENTS

I want to begin by thanking my husband, JR, for his continuous love, support, and encouragement. For reading every early draft, saying just the things I needed to hear, and giving me that little push when needed, thank you! I also want to thank my boys, Tomás and Pedro, whose encouragement ranged from "You are *still* writing that book?" to "Mami, you got this!" and whose unexpected discussion of *Latinx* took me completely by surprise and reminded me that what we call ourselves remains a topic of discussions that must continue. JR, Tomás, and Pedro, *mis tres varones, los quiero.*

Having been an elementary teacher for 17 years and moving to higher education, I wondered what I would do without a classroom of my own. But then I met Tammy Frierson, Mary Jade Haney, and María del Rocío Herron, three amazing teacher leaders and true believers in the power of children and families, who have made me a part of their school communities, and I am forever grateful. Working as we do in classrooms and with families is not possible without the support of administrators. Dr. Sabina Mosso-Taylor and Ms. Parthenia Satterwhite lend their support with a resounding, "It is for the children, yes, we can do that," to which Ms. Satterwhite often adds, "Yes, and don't forget my families."

I am grateful to all the children I have had the privilege to teach and learn alongside over the years, especially the children of Blessed Sacrament School in Jamaica Plain, Massachusetts, who taught me how to be a teacher and ignited in me a love of Latinx literature.

I am grateful, too, to the Latina mothers whom I have had the pleasure to work alongside. Their strength and determination in the face of adversity is to be admired and respected.

My fellow members of the Worlds of Words community and I are linked by our love and passion for children's literature. Thank you, WOW, and Dr. Kathy G. Short for pushing my thinking.

Doctoras Alma Flor Ada and Sonia Nieto, you have (unknowingly) served as mentors. Your work has always spoken to me. Dra. Ada, I am grateful for the close read of the manuscript, which was unexpected and so appreciated. Dra. Nieto, I am so humbled by and appreciative of the beautiful foreword you wrote.

Thank you to Lois Bridges who sought me out and encouraged this project for many years, and to Ray Coutu and the team at Scholastic who helped make this book a reality!

Finally, to the memory of my parents, Lázaro and Ana Rosa López, who loved me, taught me to stand up for what I believe in, and challenged me to exceed the low expectations set by an educational system that wasn't designed for me and others like me. *Pa'lante, pa'lante, pa'tras ni pa' coger impulso.*

Foreword by Sonia Nieto

As a fourth-grade teacher some 50 years ago, I would have been thrilled to find this book. At the time, I was teaching in the first fully bilingual school in the Northeast. Almost all my students were bilingual speakers, but there were few appropriate books for them to read in Spanish, and children's books about them were largely nonexistent. Going back even further, as a Puerto Rican child born and raised in New York City and educated in public schools, I never once saw a book by, about, or for Latin@s*. That was one of the reasons that, years later when I became a professor, I decided to focus my research largely on Puerto Rican children's literature. Like Julia López-Robertson, I wanted to make my students and their communities visible, to encourage them to feel pride in their identities—including their bilingualism—and to let them know they mattered. That is a message all children need to hear in the schools they attend, in the curriculum they learn, and in the books they read, but it is still often elusive for Latin@s.

Imagine my delight, then, in seeing this beautiful book. It has much to offer readers, whether they are teachers, teacher educators, librarians, or families. Teachers will love the many pedagogical suggestions it contains, and teacher educators will appreciate the comprehensive coverage of children's books. The fact that Julia López-Robertson, a classroom teacher for many years before becoming a university professor, retains a close working relationship with public school teachers makes it even more useful for practitioners. The book will also be treasured by librarians, who are always on the lookout for good books. López-Robertson says she wants her book "to provide *esperanza* to the multitude of Latinx children in our classrooms." And hope is exactly what so many of our children need in a world, and in schools, where they are often overlooked or misunderstood. But she also makes clear that Latin@ children's literature is not just for Latin@ students, but also for other children to learn about their Latin@ peers through realistic and authentic depictions of them.

One is struck, first of all, by the colorful and welcoming appearance of the book. What teacher wouldn't be excited to open its pages? Written with great respect for the communities it reflects, *Celebrating Our Cuentos* includes

*Latin@ is a gender-neutral, nonbinary alternative to *Latino* or *Latina*.

extensive descriptions and illustrations of some of the best children's books with Latin@ themes and characters. It is chock-full of stories of classrooms, communities, and homes. Beginning with her own story as a bilingual teacher, López-Robertson includes classroom vignettes, descriptions of home visits to her students' families, and even conversations with her own parents and children.

The introduction and first three chapters are foundational, exploring the history of Latin@s in U.S. education, our invisibility in books and school curricula, the tremendous diversity in our community, the economic inequities in the nation, instructional inequities in schools, and the significance of bilingual education, among other key topics. Particularly compelling sections explore common misconceptions about Latin@ students, and suggestions for viewing them through an asset-based lens rather than, as is often the case, a deficit-based one.

In subsequent chapters, readers are treated to innovative ways the books can be used. The pedagogical suggestions—including book talks, culturally based *pláticas*, text sets, and other imaginative ideas for using the books across the curriculum—are certain to be among teachers' favorite features. There are also heartwarming suggestions for promoting family engagement, as well as respect and understanding between schools and the communities they serve.

The book also addresses social issues, engaging teachers and students in actions they can take to create change. López-Robertson makes clear that not all children's books with Latin@ themes and characters are culturally appropriate, and she provides tools for helping teachers decide on ones that are. The final chapter recognizes effectively that children are concerned not only with good stories, but also with social justice in their classrooms, communities, and the world.

Consistently positive and affirming, *Celebrating Our Cuentos* is a splendid resource that readers will turn to time and again for ideas, inspiration, and support. It is sure to find a grateful audience among teachers and others who have been waiting for a book that celebrates Latin@ students and literature.

Sonia Nieto
Professor Emerita
College of Education
University of Massachusetts, Amherst

Dime en español/ Tell Me in Spanish

Learning How to Teach

I am the daughter of immigrants. My mother came to the United States from Colombia and my father from Cuba. Both came to the United States to pursue a better life and seek opportunities that were unavailable to them in their home countries. My parents believed in the possibilities that this nation offered them and the several family members that joined them. All of them worked hard. My mother believed that we always had to have hope because "*la esperanza nos mantiene*/hope sustains us." My hope is that this book stirs *esperanza* in you for Latinx children and all the possibilities for them in our schools and communities. I will show you how to choose Latinx children's literature wisely and weave it into your curriculum to help you help all your students reach their full potential.

(top) My parents, Lázaro and Ana Rosa López

(bottom) My mother, then Ana Rosa Viasus, with the Colombian flag

My Story

I was 23 years old when I walked into the first classroom that I would call mine. It was at Blessed Sacrament Grammar School, a school with which I had a personal connection. My parents had sacrificed and saved to enroll me and my siblings in that very same school, the neighborhood Catholic school, and now I was back as a teacher. Like many Latinos, we were raised to value hard work, respect our elders and family, and give back to the community. While no one told me to teach at Blessed Sacrament, I felt obligated to help my community and committed to providing the school's families with *esperanza* for their children.

I was 23 years old when I walked into the first classroom that I would call mine.... My newly minted degree in elementary education with a concentration in mathematics and science had prepared me well— or so I thought.

Although that was longer ago than I wish to admit, I remember it like it was yesterday. Twenty-five children looked up at me on that first morning and I was supposed to teach them everything from phonics, English (at the time reading was called "English"), math, science, religion, and the arts. My newly minted degree in elementary education with a concentration in mathematics and science had prepared me well—or so I thought.

The school was about 80 percent Latinx. Most of my students looked and sounded like me and my siblings as children. As a first grader, like my students, I entered Blessed Sacrament as an emergent bilingual, learning English at school while speaking and maintaining Spanish at home. I use the term "emergent bilingual" because it focuses on children's "evolving bilingualism" (García, Kleifgen & Falchi, 2008) rather than the term "English language learner," which places English "in a sole position of legitimacy" (García, et. al, 2008). Of my 25 students, only two were monolingual English speakers. As such, I quickly realized how unprepared I was. As a preservice teacher, I had received no training in working with emergent bilingual children, and I was not alone. Although most of my colleagues tried to work effectively with the children, none had the training or knowledge to teach them English, while at the same time holding onto their Spanish. As one of them expressed to me, "If you just graduated without knowing about how to teach emergent bilingual children, how would we have known when we graduated years ago?"

Learning How to Teach

In an effort to figure out what to do and how to teach the children, I found myself doing a lot of explaining in Spanish. When the children did not understand what I was saying in English, I said it in Spanish. If the children were unable to answer questions in English, I simply told them, *"Dime en español"/*"Tell me in Spanish." We spent our days speaking in English and Spanish all day, every day. The children were engaged and learning in two languages, and I had no idea at the time that what they were getting was a bilingual education!

About two months into the school year, my principal informed me that, based on her observations of my teaching, she had submitted my name to participate in a Diocesan pilot initiative called the Intercultural Training and Resource Center (ITRC). The mission of the ITRC was to provide teachers with resources and support for working with children from diverse cultural, socioeconomic, and linguistic backgrounds. The director, a former classroom teacher from Eastern Europe, was knowledgeable in whole-language teaching and multicultural teaching, concepts that were new to me. With several other teachers, I attended workshops twice a month that focused on strategies for engaging diverse students and for creating effective lesson plans. At the ITRC, I received the necessary support and resources to work more effectively with the children. However, I still felt something was missing.

The Daily Read-Aloud

I read aloud to my students every day. I would start the day with a poem, read aloud a book after lunch, and continue reading aloud at the end of the day. (Usually, I shared a picture book, but sometimes I shared a chapter book such as *Charlotte's Web.*) When words, phrases, or ideas were beyond the children's grasp, I translated or explained them in Spanish, enlisting the children's help.

At an ITRC workshop, the director focused on the importance of reading aloud to children and read a book in Spanish to us. That was it! I finally pinpointed what I was missing from my teaching—reading aloud books in Spanish! Prior to that workshop, I would read books in English and do on-the-spot translations to Spanish to ensure the children were grasping concepts and following story lines. Sitting in that workshop and listening to a picture book being read in Spanish was something completely revolutionary to me. Here I was, a twentysomething classroom teacher, and I had *never* seen a children's picture book in Spanish. I had absolutely no idea that such a thing existed! Immediately after the read-aloud, I asked the director if I could borrow the book to read to my students.

The book that forever changed my professional life was *Mr. Sugar Came to Town/La visita del Sr. Azúcar* (Rhomer, Gómez & Chagoya, 1989), the story of how Grandma Lupe convinces Mr. Sugar to teach her grandchildren the importance of eating a balanced diet and limiting sweets.

Mr. Sugar Came to Town/La visita del Sr. Azúcar: The Catalyst

I walked into the classroom the next morning full of excitement and anticipation, still in a lovely state of shock over the fact that I had discovered a picture book in Spanish in the United States. I gathered the children on the carpet and told them that I had found the most wonderful book to share with them. I showed them the cover, and immediately one child shouted, "It has Spanish!" Indeed, it did. Not only was the title in both Spanish and English, but every page in the book was, too. The expressions on the children's faces, as well as their reactions as I read aloud, are forever etched in my memory— squeals of delight, laughter, and joyful discussion, so much discussion!

That was the day I learned firsthand how important and necessary it is to engage all children in books that reflect their language, culture, and life experiences. Sharing this book helped me feel more confident as a teacher. For the first time, I felt I was doing the best I could for my students. I read the book in Spanish and English to ensure that each of my students was hearing the language he or she needed. After a few days of enjoying and engaging with the book, I invited the children to create a big book of *Mr. Sugar Came to Town/La visita del Sr. Azúcar*. We now had the trade book and our class-made big book, which became a well-loved addition to our class library.

The cover of and a page from a book
my class made over 30 years ago

El Sr. Azúcar and the "Home Visit"

Sra. Valderrama: *¿Cómo es posible que no haya libros en español aquí si en nuestros países los hay?*

Julia: *No sé. Cuando yo era niña, en la escuela nunca había libros en español. Este librito,* La visita del Sr. Azúcar, *es el primero que yo he visto. La semana pasada cuando fui al taller, la directora me lo enseñó. Se lo pedí prestado para leerlo a los niños.*

Sra. Valderrama: *Sería el día que lo leyó, Alejandro llegó a la casa y no hablaba de nada más que del librito, algo de un señor de azúcar y una abuela.*

Julia: *¡Sí, ese es libro! Usted se imagina la risa y felicidad cuando leí el libro.*

Sra. Valderrama: *¡Cómo no, si en todo el camino a casa se lo pasó hablando del libro y dijo que no quería postre después de la cena esa noche!*

☀

Mrs. Valderrama: How is it possible that there are no books in Spanish here if we have them in the countries we came from?

Julia: I do not know. When I was young, there were no books in Spanish. This book, *Mr. Sugar Came to Town/La visita del Sr. Azúcar,* was the first one I saw. Last week, when I was at a workshop, the director showed me the book. I asked to borrow it to read to the kids.

Mrs. Valderrama: I know the day you read it because Alejandro arrived home and did nothing but talk about it—something about a man selling sweets and a grandmother.

Julia: Yes, that is the book. You can imagine the children's laughter and joy when I read the book.

Mrs. Valderrama: Oh, of course I can! All he did the whole way home was talk about the book, and he even said he did not want dessert after dinner that night!

This discussion was from what would be my first home visit during my second year of teaching. (I had no idea at the time that what I was doing was a "home visit.") I knew Sra. Valderrama well because I had taught her older son, Roberto, the year before, my very first year of teaching. At dismissal time, the children would gather their belongings and line up, and we would walk to the front of the school building where their parents, grandparents, or older siblings were waiting for them. It was a long walk and, with 25 first graders, ours was usually the last class to arrive.

Most afternoons, parents would chat with me about homework, things going on in school, or concerns they had. One afternoon, Sra. Valderrama asked me if I had ever eaten authentic Puerto Rican food, specifically *arroz con gandules y pernil* (rice and beans with roasted pork shoulder). I told her that my Cuban father cooked *pernil* but that I had never tried the Puerto Rican version. Smiling, she said, *"Qué bien. Ven a casa para que lo puedas probar y me dices cuál prefieres el de tu papi o el mío"*/"Oh good. Come to my house to try it [*pernil*] and let me know which you prefer, your dad's or mine." I could see the expressions on Roberto and Alejandro's faces like it was yesterday—sheer terror that asked, "Why are you inviting my teacher to my house?!"

A few days later, I went to the Valderramas' for dinner. I am not sure who was more nervous, me or the children! During dinner we talked about our families, neighborhood goings-on, and school. Sra. Valderrama commented on how much Alejandro loved *La visita del Sr. Azúcar*. The Valderrama family made me feel so welcome and appreciated my bringing Spanish children's books to share with the children, which boosted my confidence. The *pernil* was delicious and, although I preferred my father's, I let Sra. Valderrama know that hers was a very close second.

El Sr. Azúcar Returns

Fast forward 30 years. (Oh my, has it been that long?!) I still visit the preK classroom of my youngest son, Pedro, who is now in high school. His former teachers, Tammy Frierson and María del Rocío Herron, have graciously invited me in over the years—and I continue to work with them and

their students. My research with young children and families would not be possible without Tammy and Rocío, who recognize that "students are disenfranchised from learning because curricula fail to capitalize on their strengths and knowledge" (López-Robertson & Haney, 2016, p. 104). They have worked with me to modify and design a curriculum that takes into account the concerns of our students and their families, with Latinx literature at the heart of our work.

Tammy Frierson (left) and María del Rocío Herron (right)

On Fridays, I engage the children in read-alouds, songs, games, and conversations about picture books, usually Latinx picture books. I have read many books to the children (which I will talk about later), including *Mr. Sugar Came to Town/La visita del Sr. Azúcar*. Recently, I was going through my bookcase preparing for a visit and came upon the book and thought, "Wow, I have not seen you in a while." I was excited to share it so many years later.

I began my read-aloud by showing the children the wonderful illustration on the back cover and asking, "What do you see?" The illustration is not large, about the size of a 4x6 inch photograph, so the children came in close and eagerly started sharing responses. "I see a grandma," said one child. "I see two kids," said another. "What is in the pot?" asked another. "I have those on my wall," observed another, pointing to the red-chili wreath. When I showed the children the book's front cover, they became really animated, "He has donuts for wheels!" "And chocolate cake in the front!" "Is that a milkshake?" As we discussed the illustration and our favorite desserts, one child pointed to the word *Azúcar*, and said, "I know that word. It is the name of that book," pointing to a book on display nearby, *¡Azúcar!* (Ivar da Coll, 2005). Because these children are immersed in multicultural and bilingual children's literature daily, they often make connections across books and notice details, such as the word *azúcar*.

I continued the read-aloud with the children chiming in at different points. They were especially concerned about the little boy who gives Abuela's tamale to the dog instead of eating it himself. They commented on the fact that they knew the Spanish words such as *abuela*, *tamal*, *azúcar*, and *niños* because they were bilingual, "just like the kids in the book." One child commented that her kitchen looked like the one in the book, sharing, "I have that painting [of *La Virgen de Guadalupe*] in my house, too. I know who that is." The children saw their homes, culture, foods, and language in the book and eagerly talked about them. After 30 years, there was still magic in *el Sr. Azúcar*!

Enhancing Curriculum With Latinx Literature

In the many years I have worked with linguistically, culturally, and socioeconomically diverse children, I have learned that sharing children's books in Spanish is important, but it is not enough. Engaging in discussions about teaching, learning, and curriculum and carrying out action-research projects led me to examine what I was teaching and what materials I was using. It did not take long for me to realize that my students' faces and life experiences were completely missing from the curriculum, which fueled my interest in using Latinx children's literature to enhance the school-provided curriculum.

For me, teaching with Latinx children's literature is both a professional and personal endeavor. As a child, I did not see myself or my experiences in any book that I read or that was read to me, and I do not want any child to feel as disconnected from school as I did. After spending three years teaching first grade and learning at the ITRC, I decided to extend my knowledge about children's literature and using it in instruction and leave my classroom to pursue a master's degree.

My coursework solidified for me the importance of creating classrooms in which children see their faces and faces like theirs, hear and tell their stories, and are encouraged to use their entire linguistic repertoire (Bartolomé, 2003; Bernal, D. D., & Alemán, 2017; García, 2009; Espinosa & Ascenzi-Moreno, 2021). As a bilingual classroom teacher for the next 14 years, I immersed myself, my students, and their families in a variety of children's literature, particularly Latinx children's literature. Because the majority of my students were bilingual Spanish/English speakers, and the majority of our families were Mexican immigrants or Mexican American, I worked to create a curriculum in which they were visible and Latinx children's literature was central.

Why This Book?

While I was able to maneuver my way through mainstream American society and school, though not without emotional scars, there are many who have not had the same opportunity. Alma Flor Ada (2015) believes that in addition to writing Latinx literature, other steps must be taken, including publication, dissemination, and awareness-building by those who can help these books reach the hands of children. I am one of those who can help Latinx children's literature reach the hands of as many children, families, and teachers as possible. Many teachers want to use Latinx children's literature but do not know where to get it, how to use it, and, most importantly, how to assess its quality. Is it well written? Is the information it contains accurate? My goal in writing this book is to provide teachers, administrators, preservice educators, and anyone working with children and families with a resource on Latinx children's literature—one that builds understanding of what it is, why it is important, and how to use it as a teaching partner.

I want this book to provide esperanza *to the multitude of Latinx children in our classrooms and to the teachers who are helping them to be successful and reach their potential.* La esperanza nos mantiene.

Most of all, I want this book to provide *esperanza* to the multitude of Latinx children in our classrooms and to the teachers who are helping them to be successful and reach their potential. *La esperanza nos mantiene*.

What You'll Find

Each chapter begins with a bilingual vignette from my life as a child in school, a classroom teacher, or as a professor of language and literacy. Throughout the book, you will find recommendations for Latinx children's literature, resources on where to find it, and suggestions for using it in your classrooms.

Chapter One

No somos invisibles/ We Are Not Invisible

Latinx People in the United States

Julia: *¡Mami, estoy aprendiendo tanto de la educación bilingüe y no se imagina cuantos libritos he leído que están escritos en español!*

Mami: *Cuando estaban en la escuela nunca tenían libros en español.*

Julia: *¡Yo sé, y no fue hasta que me mandaron a los talleres de la escuela que yo supe que existían! Las directoras me los prestan y los leo en la clase, y cómo los disfrutamos.*

Mami: *Yo te veo traduciendo las notas para los padres, qué bien que haces eso, hija. Nunca mandaban nada en español. Uno como que se siente invisible.*

☀

Julia: Mami, I am learning so much about bilingual education, and you can't imagine the number of [children's] books that I am reading in Spanish!

Mami: When you and your siblings were in school, you never had books in Spanish.

Julia: I know, and it wasn't until I was sent to these workshops that I even knew they existed in the United States. The director lent me the books, and I read them in class, and we enjoy them so.

Mami: I see you translating notices for your families. How good that you do that, daughter. Your school never sent anything home in Spanish. You feel like you are invisible.

I lived at home when I began teaching, and my mother and I spoke often at dinner about my experiences. We talked about my students, field-trip plans (I have always loved field trips), and similarities and differences between being a former student and a current teacher in the same school. Although those conversations happened many, many years ago, they have stuck with me, particularly the one above. "Feeling invisible"? No one should ever feel invisible—or, to quote Maya González, Chicana author, educator, and activist, from an anonymous graffiti artist she saw in the Mission District in San Francisco, CA, "A people should not long for their own image" (retrieved from mayagonzalez.com/artist/bio). As the Latinx population in the United States grows, it is critical to make Latinx images part of the everyday classroom life.

Neither we nor our children should long to see our images in our classrooms and curriculum.

In this chapter, I discuss the importance of a name—is it *Hispanic*, *Latino*, or *Latinx*—and explain my choice of terms both for myself and for the book title. This chapter also includes a brief discussion of important legislation that continues to impact Latinx students in U.S. schools.

What's in a Name?

Over the years, there have been many terms used to describe the Spanish-speaking population: *Hispanic, Latino, Mexican, Latino Americans, Spanish-Americans, Spanish-speaking Americans, Latin@,* and more recently, *Latinx*. As such, in this section, I provide brief definitions of some of those terms, indicate the ones I use in this book, and explain why. Please understand that this is a serious topic that goes well beyond the scope of this book. My explanations are brief, but thorough—and mean no disrespect to anyone who chooses to use different terms. There is power in choosing what to be called. As Jorge J. E. Gracia (2000) offers, "some names disempower those who have them in ways that have serious repercussions throughout their lives." For that reason, when deciding on terms to use in your practice, be sure to consult your students and their families about their preferences.

During the Nixon administration, from 1969 to 1974, the United States government used *Hispanic* as a way to account for the Spanish-speaking population in the census, defining that population as "people of Central or South American, Cuban, Mexican, Puerto Rican, or other Spanish culture or origin, regardless of race" (census.gov). Prior to that, the census categorized the Spanish-speaking population as "white." The new designation provided data to identify and reduce inequities in education, housing, and funding.

Latino is used to describe a person of Latin American, Spanish-speaking origin—or, as Ellen Riojas Clark and Belinda Bustos Flores say, "a citizen of the U.S. with Latin American roots" (2016). Often, the terms *Latino* and *Hispanic* are used interchangeably. However, according to Cristina González and Patricia Gándara (2005), there is a significant distinction between them: "Hispanic was an imposition from above, an invention of the Census Bureau, whereas *Latino* was an autonomous alternative to the official nomenclature."

Some Spanish-speaking people prefer *Latino* because it captures ethnic pride and suggests the wide-ranging mix of Latin American people, while they associate Hispanic with Spanish colonization and conquest.

According to Cristobal Salinas (2020), *Latinx* originated in higher education in an effort to include all gender identities. While the term is gaining popularity with academics and activists, *Latinx* is not accepted by all; some believe it is simply a "buzzword and a blatant form of linguistic imperialism that is being used only in the United States" (Salinas & Lozano, 2019). Others, however, view *Latinx* as a "meaningful and transformative word that promotes gender inclusivity, and thus a respect for basic human dignity" (Salinas & Lozano, 2019). While DeGuzmán (2017) adds that *Latinx* is primarily used within the United States and territories, the Pew Hispanic Center (2020) offers that "only 23% of U.S. adults who self-identify as Hispanic or Latino have heard of the term *Latinx*, and just 3% say they use it to describe themselves."

I self-identify as *Latina*, the term commonly used to describe a female of Latin American, Spanish-speaking origin. My Cuban-born father self-identified as *Cubano* and *Hispano*, while my

Countries of Origin of Our Latinx Students and Their Families

Colombian-born mother self-identified as *Colombiana* and *Latina*. Yet, both used the terms *Hispano* and *Latino* interchangeably. Most Latinos I know prefer to identify according to their country of origin (e.g., Cuban, Colombian, Mexican, Dominican).

Given the sheer number of terms, it is not easy to choose one when working with children and their families. It is always best and more respectful to simply ask them their preference. If they are too young to know, speak with their parents.

I use *Latinx* throughout this book to identify people with roots in Spanish-speaking countries who live in the United States and who may or may not speak Spanish. When I use the terms *Latina*, *Latino*, or the country of origin, it is because the person to whom I am referring has self-identified as such. Likewise, if the term *Hispanic* is used, it is because the data I am reporting has used the term. As I noted at the beginning of this section, this topic deserves much more discussion than what I have provided; my intention was to clarify my stance for the use of the term *Latinx* and offer some insight into the issue.

The Pew Hispanic Center reported that in 2019 there were nearly 60.6 million Latinx people living in the United States, making up 18 percent of the total population. Because the greatest number of Latinx immigrants in the United States are of Mexican origin, there is an erroneous presumption that if one is Latinx, one is Mexican. But Latinx people in the United States represent many areas, including México, Puerto Rico, Cuba, El Salvador, Dominican Republic, Guatemala, and Colombia—and each group carries its own cultural nuances, traditions, language variations, history, ways of interacting with the environment, and ways of identifying. Viewing Latinx people as monocultural and homogenous can lead to stereotyping and bias.

Picture Books That Capture Diversity in the Latinx Community

While we share the same language, as well as a commitment to our families and communities, *no somos lo mismo*/we are not all the same. Here are some books that capture diversity in the Latinx community.

De aquí como el coquí/Coquí in the City (2021) by Nomar Pérez (2021). Miguel and his parents are moving from Puerto Rico to the U.S. mainland, which means he is leaving behind his grandparents and *coquí*, a species of frog found in Puerto Rico.

Islandborn (2018) by Junot Díaz. This is the lovely story of how a community helped a little girl remember "the Island" (Dominican Republic) where she was born.

All the Way to Havana (2017) by Margarita Engle. This is the story of a little boy and his parents driving from the Cuban countryside to Havana in their old car for a family celebration. Beautiful illustrations let the reader see what present-day Havana looks like.

Digging for Words: José Alberto Gutiérrez and the Library He Built (2020) by Angela Burke Kunkel is the story of a garbage collector in Bogotá, Colombia, who creates a much-needed library for his community from the books he finds.

Rainbow Weaver/Tejedora del arcoíris (2016) by Linda Elovitz Marshall and illustrator Elisa Chavarri. Ixchel wants to learn how to weave like her mother and grandmother, but they are busy preparing their weavings to take to market. So Ixchel comes up with an idea. She collects and washes the plastic bags strewn all over her Guatemalan town, cuts them into strips, and weaves them into a colorful fabric that looks like a beautiful rainbow, just like the weavings of Mayan women before her.

My Papi Has a Motorcycle (2019) by Isabel Quintero tells the story of a Mexican American girl, Daisy, and the joy she feels riding around her ever-changing community on her papi's motorcycle.

Latinx Children in U.S. Public Schools

According to the National Center for Education Statistics (NCES), the population of Latinx children in American public schools continues to climb. From fall 2000 to fall 2017, enrollment rose from 16 percent to 27 percent, while during the same period, the percent of white students decreased. NCES reported that, in the 2019–2020 school year, of the 56.5 million students attending public school, 13.9 million were Hispanic (the term used by NCES). The population of Latinx school-aged children is predicted to reach 15.5 million by the year 2024 and will represent 29 percent of the total school population.

Logically, the school curriculum would reflect the changing demographic, but that is often not the case. In fact, "Latino literature and the life experiences of Latino children are typically not made a part of school learning" (López-Robertson, 2010). As a result, Latinx children too often feel they are not valued members of school communities, have no contributions to make, and are outsiders in their own classrooms (Delgado Bernal, 2000; Nieto, 2010; Suárez-Orozco & Suárez-Orozco, 2001; Valdés, 1996; Valenzuela, 1999). Very often, those feelings are perpetuated by educators who see Latinx students, especially those learning English, as an obstacle rather than as an asset (Bucholz, Casillas & Lee, 2017; Nieto, 2001; Reyes & Halcón, 2001). However, Latinx students do not require extra time from their teachers; just like all students, they require the support of their teachers coupled with high expectations, and they need to see themselves represented in the curriculum.

Latinx Schooling in the United States: A Short History

Latinx students have not fared well in U.S. public schools and continue to "survive a history of institutional neglect" (Yosso, 2006), dating back to the early 1900s. Historically, educators have sought to subordinate Latinx students by providing them with limited access to inferior, non-academic instruction (Davila, Michaels, Hurtado, Roldan & Duran-Graybow, 2016; Delgado Bernal, 2000; Gándara, 2008, 1995). Unfortunately, bilingual education has become a political hot topic related to issues of race, poverty, and immigration. Through the years, there have been several court cases related to the right of Latinx students to receive a quality education. Let us look at some of those cases to gain a fuller picture of Latinx schooling in the United States today.

Alvarez v. Lemon Grove School District (1931). In the summer of 1931, in eastern San Diego, the Lemon Grove School Board approved the construction of a two-room schoolhouse to segregate Mexican children, under pressure by members of the white community. The parents of the children impacted by the decision formed the Comité de Vecinos de Lemon Grove (Lemon Grove Neighborhood Committee) and, together with the greater Mexican American community, sued the school district. Although legal precedence was not set because it was viewed as a local event, the Lemon Grove Incident was the first successful class-action lawsuit to end school desegregation. *All Equal: A Ballad of Lemon Grove/Todos iguales: Un corrido de Lemon Grove* (2019) by Christy Hale tells the story in *corrido* format, a traditional Mexican story song.

Méndez v. Westminster (1946). The Méndez family moved to Westminster, a small town in Southern California, where only white students were admitted to school. Gonzalo Méndez sent his children, including his daugher Sylvia, with his sister, Soledad Vidaurri, and her children to register them at the Westminster elementary school, where she was told that her children could attend, but the Méndez children could not, because her children had lighter skin and a French-origin last name. Soledad was told that her brother's children needed to attend the Mexican school nearby. With a group of other parents, Gonzalo hired a civil rights attorney, sued four Orange County school districts, and won the case, making illegal school segregation of children of Mexican origin. Because of that decision, the Ninth Circuit Appeals Court established a national precedent for the termination of segregated "Mexican schools." In the decision, Judge Paul J. McCormick noted, "a paramount requisite in the American system of public education is social equality. It must be open to all children by unified school association regardless of lineage." *Méndez v. Westminster* laid the groundwork for *Brown v. Board of Education* and is the subject of the book Separate *Is Never Equal: Sylvia Méndez and Her Family's Fight for Desegregation* by Duncan Tonatiuh, 2015.

Brown v. Board of Education (1954). While the Méndez case made it illegal to segregate children of Mexican origin, the law was rarely enforced. In 1951, the NAACP filed a class-action lawsuit on behalf of Oliver Brown and other families challenging racial segregation in Topeka, Kansas, schools. In 1954, the Supreme Court, under Chief Justice Earl Warren, noted that separate was inherently unequal and ruled that the plaintiffs were being "deprived of the equal protection of the laws guaranteed by the 14th Amendment."

Bilingual Education Act (1968). The Bilingual Education Act, Title VII, signaled the federal government's recognition of the unique needs of non-English speaking children in American schools. It provided federal funding through grants for schools to create innovative programs to teach English to students who needed it and improve their educational experiences. However, it did not recognize the benefits or importance of bilingualism or the links between language and culture, instead suggesting that non-English-speaking students were "problems" needing to be "fixed."

Lau v. Nichols (1974). In 1971, the San Francisco Unified School District (SFUSD) desegregated, as required by law, and about 3,000 Chinese students were enrolled in schools throughout the district, but only a fraction of students needing supplementary English language instruction received it. The Office for Civil Rights established Lau Remedies, guidelines for school districts to provide a meaningful education to students developing English proficiency, which led to the creation of bilingual and other supplementary programs in most public schools.

California Proposition 227 (1998). The intention of this proposition, sponsored by Ron Unz, a Silicon Valley software entrepreneur, was to educate English learners in a one-year program and eliminate most of the multiyear programs. The proposition passed but was repealed in 2016.

Arizona Proposition 203 or English for the Children (2000). Prior to 2000, schools in Arizona were free to determine the best type of instruction for their English learners. This proposition limited the type of instruction available to them, arguing that English learners should be educated effectively and quickly in immersion programs lasting no more than one year. The proposition passed by 63 percent of the vote, demonstrating Arizona's support of assimilation over multiculturalism.

Ongoing Challenges for Latinx Children at School

The American public education system has a dual nature (Darder & Torres, 2014). First, it is "market-driven and reproduces class relations of power and inequality." Students are assimilated into mainstream cultural values through the hidden curriculum offered by schools where they learn to accept "existing social and material conditions of inequality" without question. Second, it is still seen as the great equalizer (Mann, 1848). The prevailing notion is that citizens have access to an education, and success is up to each of us. The challenges of Latinx children are often due to factors outside their control, and often related to economic, instructional, social, and academic inequities.

The challenges of Latinx children are often due to factors outside their control, and often related to economic, instructional, social, and academic inequities.

Economic Inequities As a whole, the Latinx community earns less than other groups and tends to depend on low-skill jobs, making it susceptible to a shifting economy (U.S. Census Bureau, 2017). Economic inequity has the potential to negatively impact children, e.g., food scarcity, homelessness.

Instructional Inequities Schools with high Latinx populations are subject to inequitable distribution of resources. Students tend to be segregated in homogenous schools that do not offer high-level or college-prep courses. Teachers are often not equipped to provide the support those students need, and because they do not have the means to send their children to private schools, Latinx families rely on public education, demonstrating that "economic vulnerability and academic achievement are inextricably linked" (Gutiérrez, Baquedano-López, & Álvarez, 2000).

Social Inequities Latinx students are often victims of meritocracy. The notion that if you work hard, you can make it implies that all people are on equal footing from the start, which is simply not true. The contexts in which students learn tend to be monolingual and monocultural, and students must deal with issues such as *linguicism*, prohibiting the use of one's home language as a tool to learning English. Movements such as "English Only" in California, Arizona, and Massachusetts privilege monolingualism. All students, regardless of their home language, should have access to a quality education and "authentic and ample opportunities to learn, including the right to use the full range of their sociocultural and linguistic resources as tools for learning" (Gutiérrez, et. al, 2000).

Academic Inequities Several factors play a role in Latinx children's academic progress. Children in high-poverty schools tend to have less qualified and/or less experienced teachers. Many teachers are not trained to work with children who speak Spanish as a first language, and there is a "history of social oppression and marginalization that continues to the present" (Ada, 2015). Spanish was the home language of 3.7 million English learners in U.S. public schools in the fall of 2017, representing 74.8 percent of all English learners and 7.6 percent of all K–12 students in U.S. public schools. Teachers' attitudes toward English learners play a huge role in shaping educational outcomes, as noted by Walker, Shafer, and Iams (2004):

> Teachers who hold negative, ethnocentric, or racist attitudes about ELLs, or who believe in any of the numerous fallacies surrounding the education of language-minority students, often fail to meet the academic and social needs of these students and work to maintain the hegemonic legitimacy of the dominant social order.

As a consequence of disparities, Latinx students are overrepresented in the data with lower educational results; they tend to have lower scores on standardized tests, lower grades in school, and higher dropout rates compared to students from other racial and ethnic groups. It is important to address those fallacies to improve the educational outcomes of our Latinx students.

Common Misconceptions About Latinx Children

In this section, I will discuss some common misconceptions about Latinx children and English learners that have historically hindered their academic success.

Misconception 1: Latinx Children Are Deficient A prevalent view is that many minoritized children, children from linguistically, culturally, and socioeconomically diverse backgrounds, come to school with deficiencies—meaning that they are missing something—which places the culpability on children and their families, without looking at systemic issues. Too often, the children are blamed for their academic underperformance. We need to "utilize the full repertoire of skills that students bring to and develop in the classroom" (Gutiérrez, et al., 2000).

Misconception 2: All Latinx Children Are English Learners According to data from the National Center for Educational Statistics (2020), in the fall of 2017, Spanish-speaking English learners made up 76.5 percent of all English learners in public schools. But despite the fact that many Latinx students are English learners, not all of them are.

Misconception 3: All Latinx Children Speak Spanish Deciding whether to speak Spanish is not a decision to make lightly. Many families fear their children will suffer discrimination as they may have when they immigrated to the United States and, as a result, decide against maintaining Spanish (López-Robertson, 2014). Additionally, many Latinx infants and toddlers who join monolingual families through adoption, foster care, etc., are raised speaking English only. Finally, some Latinx children do not feel confident speaking Spanish because they are being raised in the U.S. surrounded by English and may not have the opportunity to speak as much Spanish as they would like, as is the case in *Stella Díaz Has Something to Say* (2018) by Angela Dominguez.

Misconception 4: Younger Children Are More Effective Language Learners Than Older Children Younger children tend to acquire language more rapidly for a few reasons. They have fewer inhibitions and will try out words and phrases because they are risk-takers. They have more opportunities for social interaction with peers, on the playground, in the classroom, in the cafeteria, and their sentence constructions and vocabulary tend to be simpler and shorter. As students progress through school, the academic and language demands become more challenging, and they must adapt to them. Older students must work with more sophisticated and abstract language than younger ones.

Misconception 5: Latinx English Learners Do Not Need Specialized Instruction English learners' exposure to English prior to entering school varies, from no exposure to a lot (Cummins, 2000; Freeman & Freeman, 2002). English learners are tasked with learning both academic content and language simultaneously. In order for them to be successful, they need support, which takes many forms, including working with an ESL teacher and having their classroom teacher provide visual aids (picture cards, realia), content vocabulary in their home language, and/or peer support.

Misconception 6: Latinx English Learners Will Learn English Faster With English-Only Instruction English immersion can have many negative effects on English learners, including eroding their sense of identity, losing proficiency in their native language, feeling marginalized by mainstream society, and causing low academic performance. English learners are usually more successful and happier when they can use their native language to learn English.

Misconception 7: Learning Two Languages in Early Childhood Confuses Children Negotiating two languages provides many benefits. Jim Cummins's (2000) additive bilingual enrichment principle suggests that there are "subtle metalinguistic and intellectual benefits for bilingual children." Learning a second language boosts problem-solving, critical thinking, listening, and multitasking.

Misconception 8: Learning a Second Language Is the Same as Learning a Native Language In his theory of Second Language Acquisition, Stephen Krashen (1992) makes the distinction between *acquiring* language and *learning* language. Acquiring language is a subconscious process; it is the way we "pick up" language as children. Learning language, on the other hand, is conscious and focused on rule- and grammar-based approaches used in schools. While they may not completely understand a second language, through *comprehensible input*, meaningful content that is supported by context and visual aids, students will acquire language naturally, rather than learn it consciously.

Building on Strengths

All children enter school with the ability to "read the world" (Freire & Macedo, 1987). We want to build on the strength and knowledge that Latinx children bring to school; they have spent their lives in their communities learning the language and the ways of being members in their community. These ways of knowing should be used as the foundation upon which to build their learning experiences.

Shift From an "Achievement Gap" to an "Opportunity Gap"

The achievement gap focuses on disparities in student outcomes, test scores, dropout rates, etc., between Latinx students and white students. The *opportunity gap*, on the other hand, focuses on issues of access Latinx students face while striving to achieve. While the achievement gap often looks at symptoms and places blame, the opportunity gap highlights the challenges students face.

View Latinx Students Through an Asset-Based Lens

Educators, counselors, administrators, and all school personnel need to view Latinx students through an asset-based lens, recognizing that they are holders and creators of knowledge (Bernal, 2002). Some schools and communities have begun to shift the paradigm and recognize Latinx students for the strengths, talents, and cultural perspectives they bring. Their language is viewed as a resource (Ruiz, 1984), priceless human capital, and a tool to "enhance cognitive skills" (Gándara, 2008). When Latinx students' language and linguistic abilities are seen as assets, they can be "exploited for their educational benefit" (Gándara, 2008)—of both the Latinx students and their peers of all backgrounds.

Capitalize on Funds of Knowledge

Many educators have used the groundbreaking work of González, Moll, and Amanti (2005) to build upon the knowledge and ways of knowing that children bring with them from their homes. Funds of knowledge are acquired through daily interactions with one's family and community members and "are essential for thriving within one's community" (López-Robertson, 2016). When funds of knowledge are seen as a strength, members of the school community are more likely to find ways for Latinx children (and other marginalized groups) to become not only successful in school, but also integral to making the community stronger. In the chapters that follow, I will occasionally touch on the role of funds of knowledge and how to uncover them in your Latinx students and use them in your teaching with Latinx literature.

When funds of knowledge are seen as a strength, members of the school community are more likely to find ways for Latinx children (and other marginalized groups) to become not only successful in school, but also integral to making the community stronger.

Concluding Thought

As a child in school, I was invisible. My school did not recognize my language or culture and, rather than view them as assets, they were viewed as things to overcome. Knowing some of the history of Latinx children in U.S. schools and being able to dispel some myths provides a more informed lens through which to view Latinx students. We are more apt to see the cultural and intellectual advantages that Latinx students bring to the school community when we learn about their history in U.S. schools. Latinx literature provides one lens through which to view and begin to learn about the Latinx community.

Chapter Two

Yo soy de allá/ That's Where I Am From

What Latinx Literature Is and Who It's for

I was engaging a group of four-year-old children in a read-aloud of *ABeCedarios: Mexican Folk Art ABCs in English and Spanish* (Weill, 2014), a book with beautiful photographs of carvings by woodworkers from Oaxaca,

Mexico. The children were on the carpet facing me, lumped together, as they always seem to end up. I showed them the back cover and then the front cover and asked them what they noticed. After a few responses, I explained to the children what the book contained, and then I began to read. All of a sudden, Miguel could not contain his excitement. He stood, walked up to me, and shouted, *"Miss, miss, eso es de mi pueblo. Eso es de Oaxaca. ¡Yo soy de allá!"*/"Miss, miss, that is from my town. That is from Oaxaca. I am from there!" I handed him the book, and his eyes lit up, a toothless smile took over his whole face. He held the book tenderly and repeated, *"¡Es de mi pueblo! ¡Es de mi pueblo! ¡Yo soy de allá!"*/"It is from my town! It is from my town. I am from there!"

All children deserve to see their language, culture, traditions, and worlds in which they live positively reflected in books in their classrooms, libraries, and communities. Holding those books in their hands, as Miguel did, makes their reality "real." If there is a book about it, someone must think it is important. Cynthia Weill, the author of *ABeCedarios*, placed value on Miguel's birthplace by making a book featuring the work of artisans from there, which enabled Miguel to see an important part of himself in its pages. As a "tool of cultural representation and a powerful resource to contest deficit beliefs about languages and cultures found in the Americas" (Clark & Flores, 2016), Latinx literature can be influential in supporting Latinx children's emerging sense of identity and pride in their language and culture. But what about non-Latinx children? Can they benefit from the literature, too? Of course!

To understand the benefits of Latinx children's literature, it is important to understand what it is and who it's for. This chapter will also delve into the different terminology used for children's literature about diverse cultures.

Children's Literature as Mirrors, Windows, and Doors

Children's literature is a powerful tool for understanding the world in which we live. It can be used to expand children's knowledge about their own culture as well as other people's cultures. Rudine Sims Bishop's (1990, 1992) seminal work asks us to consider children's literature as a mirror, a window, and a sliding glass door. As a mirror, children's literature serves to affirm children and their communities—it "connects one's experience to larger discourses concerning power, society, and sociohistorical tensions" (Bishop, 1990). As a window, literature allows children to see others and try to understand another's experience, and as a sliding glass door, "readers have only to walk through in imagination to become part of whatever world has been created and recreated by the author" (Bishop, 1990).

Children's literature is a powerful tool for understanding the world in which we live. It can be used to expand children's knowledge about their own culture as well as other people's cultures.

When I was a child, reading was not something that I chose to do. I saw it as a chore and did it because I had to, until my fifth-grade teacher, Sister MaryAnn Tracy, brought it to life for me. She read aloud to us every day after lunch, and she loved it. She read with expression, often cracking herself up and laughing out loud. I recall some of the titles she shared: *Charlotte's Web*, *The Hundred Dresses*, and *The Borrowers*, and while I did not have much in common with the characters in those books, I believe that I connected with them because I was surrounded by storytelling at home, and enjoyed listening to stories being read aloud. I was unaware of the fact that I *should* see myself in books and, as a result, never *expected* to see myself in books. Was I so fully assimilated in the educational system that I was oblivious to the fact that "reducing *my* opportunities to learn about and to appreciate my own cultural heritage runs contrary to *my* basic educational rights" (Ada, 2016, emphasis added)? Does it matter that I was not represented in books? Of course it does. Should it matter? Of course it should!

Cuentos Matter

Kathy Short and Dana Fox (2003) remind us that "stories do matter to children; they influence the ways in which children think about themselves and their place in the world as well as the ways in which they think about other cultural perspectives and peoples." Without seeing myself or my cultural background in books, my desire to read was limited. There were no mirrors for me. No books reflected any part of my existence. I was surrounded by windows.

I do not want children to feel invisible in school. I do not want them to feel unwelcome. I want them to feel pride in their linguistic capabilities—in the fact that they may be bilingual, code switchers, and language brokers. Those capabilities should be celebrated and used as the foundation for teaching and learning. I want children to connect personally with books in their classrooms, libraries, and homes; to see their lives, experiences, and languages in the pages of those books. I want all children to have experiences similar to Miguel's with *ABeCedarios*. I want them to be able to hold onto the concrete representation of their culture, to hear their language being read, and to share it with their classmates and community.

Enter Latinx Children's Literature

Engaging children with diverse literature helps them understand that everyone has a story to tell and that those stories are to be valued and appreciated. It nurtures and infuses an appreciation of all people as valued and significant individuals and prepares them for life in our global society. The literature must be carefully selected and, as Alma Flor Ada (2003) reminds us:

> Children and youth should have access to the best of their culture and the universal human culture. To be meaningful, their education needs to include the best of what has been created specifically for them, and high-quality literature, rich and diverse, needs to have a central place in the education of children and youth.

Children have the right to see themselves represented in quality literature that is shared in their schools and communities.

The Latinx community has a long history in the United States. Much of Latinx literature is infused with that history, capturing challenges and conflicts, joys and victories. In Flores, Clark, and Smith's (2016) words, it contains "culturally specific practices, traditions, customs, folk beliefs, and mythologies that often serve as the basis for themes in Latino literature." The linguistic diversity in the Latinx community is also captured in the choices authors make. For example, some Latinx literature is written in English, some in Spanish, and some bilingually in Spanish and English. Some books are written almost entirely in one language, with words and phrases in the other language sprinkled throughout the text. (In Chapter Three, I address issues of authenticity of the use of Spanish.) Latinx children's literature captures the pluralism of most U.S. public schools and communities, and of society, and as such, it needs to be in classrooms.

María del Rocío Herron reads aloud to her students.

A Brief History of Latinx Children's Literature in the U.S.

Latinx children's literature is deeply rooted in the oral tradition. The first Spanish speakers to arrive in the Americas carried with them folktales, myths, legends, nursery rhymes, tongue twisters and *adivinanzas* (riddles) that are still around today. Some (Ada, 2016; 2003; Campoy & Ada, 2011) trace the origins of Latinx children's literature to the writings of José Martí. In 1889, while exiled from Cuba and living in New York, he published *La edad de oro* (*The Golden Age*), a literary magazine written for and dedicated to Spanish-speaking children living in the Americas. The magazine was pivotal because it recognized the child as reader. Although only four issues were published, they were gathered into one book that remains popular today. That book, according to F. Isabel Campoy and Alma Flor Ada, marked the "beginning of written Latino children's literature" (2011).

José Martí, the Father of Latinx Children's Literature

Martí did not talk down to children or shy away from social issues. His writing condemns oppression and discrimination, with the hope that "young people will embrace the concept of equality among all human beings and espouse justice as the means for living in a world at peace" (Campoy & Ada, 2011). In *Los zapaticos de rosa*, for example, Martí deals with issues of poverty and classism.

The poem first appeared in the magazine *La edad de oro* and later became a book illustrated by Puerto Rican author/illustrator Lulu Delacre. It is about a little girl, Pilar, who comes from a wealthy family. While visiting the beach, she notices that the ocean is more active by the bluffs, so she asks her mother permission to go play there. Her mother approves but warns her to avoid letting her *zapaticos de rosa*/pink shoes get wet. Pilar agrees and heads to the bluffs. After a while she returns without the shoes. Just as her mother is about to scold her, a woman interrupts them. She explains that her little girl is ill and that, while playing, Pilar noticed that she had no shoes, so she gave her the *zapaticos de rosa*. Pilar's mother is overjoyed to learn of her daughter's act of kindness and embraces her.

Martí wanted children to be aware of issues of injustice, to live in a world of peace and equality, and to embrace "social activism and community building that have been a part of Latino/a literary history from its earliest moments" (González, 2009).

Latinx Literature's Emergence in the 1970s

The emergence of Latinx children's literature as we know it today can be traced back to the 1970s. During the Civil Rights era, the Latinx community became more active. Latinx writers for adults began "chronicling their experiences growing up Latina/o in the United States" (González, 2009), providing an unprecedented look into the community. In the 1970s, books for children and young adults started appearing. Nuyorican writer Nicholasa Mohr wrote several celebrated titles, including *Nilda* (1973), *El Bronx Remembered* (1975), *In Nueva York* (1977), and *Felita* (1979). Rudolfo Anaya, often referred to as the father of Chicano literature, wrote *Bless Me, Ultima* (1972), a critically acclaimed book that was adapted and released as a feature film in 2013.

Legislation mandating schools to offer materials in Spanish to Spanish-speaking students prompted the publishing industry to produce more Latinx children's literature. Until then, most materials in Spanish were imported from publishers outside the U.S. from companies such as Santillana and Ediciones Ekaré. Small publishing houses, such as *Arte Público Press* in Houston (1979) and *Cinco Puntos Press* in El Paso (1985), started cropping up in the U.S. Children's Book Press, founded in 1975 with a grant from the U.S. Department of Education, was the country's first publishing house to focus on quality bilingual and multicultural children's literature. In 2011, it was sold to Lee & Low Books, which offers multicultural children's literature, including bilingual English/Spanish titles.

Latinx Literature's Coming of Age in the 1990s

Latinx children's literature, as we now know it today, came of age in the 1990s when noted Latinx authors began to write for children and adolescents.

Those authors included Alma Flor Ada (*Gathering the Sun: An Alphabet in Spanish and English* [1997], *La moneda de oro* [1991], *Querido Pedrín/Dear Peter Rabbit* [1994]); Pat Mora (*A Birthday Basket for Tía* [1992], *Listen to the Desert* [1994], *Confetti* [1996], *Tomás and the Library Lady* [1997]); and Gary Soto (*Baseball in April* [1990], *Too Many Tamales/¡Qué montón de tamales!* [1992], *Chato's Kitchen* [1997]).

As Latinx literature gained popularity, book awards were created specifically for it. The Américas Award for Children's and Young Adult Literature, established in 1993 by the national Consortium of Latin American Studies Programs (CLASP), recognizes books that authentically portray Latin America, the Caribbean, or Latinx in the United States (claspprograms.org/americasaward).

The Pura Belpré Award, established in 1996 and named for Pura Belpré, the first Latina librarian at the New York Public Library, is co-sponsored by the Association for Library Service to Children (ALSC) and REFORMA, the National Association to Promote Library and Information Services to Latinos and the Spanish-Speaking. It is presented annually to a "Latinx writer and illustrator whose work best portrays, affirms, and celebrates the Latino cultural experience in an outstanding work of literature for children and youth (ala.org/alsc/awardsgrants/bookmedia/belpremedal).

Planting Stories: The Life of Librarian and Storyteller Pura Belpré (2019) and the Spanish edition, *Sembrando historias: Pura Belpré: bibliotecaria y narradora de cuentos* (2019) by Anika A. Denise and illustrated by Paola Escobar, tells Pura

Belpré's story beautifully. Belpré began writing children's books in the 1930s. Her goal was to preserve and disseminate Puerto Rican folklore. Her first book, *Pérez and Martina: A Portorican Folk Tale,* was published in 1932 and, in 1965, a collection of tales titled *The Tiger and the Rabbit and Other Tales,* illustrated by Tomie dePaola, became the first English collection of Puerto Rican folk tales published in the United States (centropr.hunter.cuny.edu/collections).

Established in 1995 at Texas State University, the Tomás Rivera Award was created to honor authors and illustrators who create literature depicting the Mexican American experience. The award is named in honor of Texas State distinguished alumnus, Dr. Tomás Rivera.

Tomás and the Library Lady and the separate Spanish edition, *Tomás y la señora de la biblioteca* (1997), written by Mexican American writer Pat Mora and illustrated by Raúl Colón, are based on Tomás Rivera's life as the son of a migrant farm worker during the 1940s in the United States.

For a complete list of awards celebrating Latinx children's literature, visit scholastic.com/CuentosResources.

The rise in Latinx children's literature in the 1990s coincided with the beginning of my classroom teaching career, my graduate studies, and my bilingual teaching experience, and, as such, I remember spending a lot of money on books! I remember fondly reading aloud *Mr. Sugar Came to Town/La visita del Sr. Azúcar* by Harriet Rhomer, *De Colores and Other Latin-American Folk Songs for Children* by José Luis Orozco, *Angel's Kite/La estrella de Ángel* by Alberto Blanco, and *Family Pictures/Cuadros de familia* by Carmen Lomas Garza, and my students eagerly sharing connections to the illustrations and stories.

De Colores and other Latin-American Folk Songs for Children (1999) by José Luis Orozco came with an audiocassette (now available on CD). I played the music and sang songs with my students, who also used them for finger plays, jump rope, and games during recess. We turned some songs into books and added them to our classroom library, and I also wrote many of the songs on chart paper and used them for shared reading.

Who Is Latinx Children's Literature For?

At the start of this chapter, I introduced you to Miguel and the joy he felt when I shared a book with him that captured a familiar place: his *pueblo*! All children should have the opportunity to feel that joy—to see something familiar in a book and make a personal connection. As celebrated Latinx author/illustrator Yuyi Morales (2016) so beautifully stated:

> The Latino child recognizes himself or herself in the stories, finds in the illustrations things that he has at home, sees foods that she eats with her family, cherishes celebrations that his loved ones taught him about, understands habits that exist within her community.

That said, the books should reflect not only children's immediate world, but also worlds beyond because learning occurs in the spaces between the known and unknown (Nieto, 1992). Latinx children's literature offers learning opportunities to Latinx and non-Latinx children.

Significance for Latinx Children

Latinx literature provides Latinx children with a mirror reflecting their languages and cultures and a window with a view to other Latinx communities. It helps them see that they are a part of a world beyond their immediate surroundings, that there are others like them, and that they are valued. It also helps them recognize that they are a part of a "continuum of creators" (Ada, 2003). What a powerful statement! With Latinx literature, Latinx children see that they, too, can be active, contributing members of society capable of great things. They develop a positive sense of self and ethnic identity, and improve their academic performance (Clark & Flores, 2001).

Sense of Self and Ethnic Identity Latinx children's literature can play a positive role in "children's understandings of how they are viewed and valued by the school and the society of which schools are reflections" (Nieto, 1997). Seeing someone with whom they can identify, someone outside of their family, in a book in school or at the library, is more important for Latinx children's developing sense of self and ethnic identity. Miguel, as you may remember, was bolstered when he recognized his pueblo in the book I shared with him. He felt valued.

Sarai and the Meaning of Awesome (2018), a series by Sarai Gonzalez and Monica Brown, is about Sarai, the daughter of a Costa Rican father and Peruvian mother. Sarai became famous in the Bomba Estéreo video for the song "*Soy, yo*" (That's Me) and came to represent positive self-worth, identity, and female empowerment. The Sarai series invites readers into the adventures of a strong young Latina.

Rigoberto González (*Soledad Sigh Sighs* [2003] and *Antonio's Card/La tarjeta de Antonio* [2005/2016]) explained the importance of seeing oneself in a book and offered that it "reflects the importance of one's cultural history and geography to one's evolving sense of self" (cited in López, 2009). *Antonio's Card* is a bilingual story about a boy from a nontraditional family. When Latinx children learn about their cultural histories and geographies, it impacts their developing ethnic identity.

Academic Performance

In my experience, when learning is meaningful and intentionally draws from their funds of knowledge, Latinx students excel. When they see their language, culture, and communities respectfully represented in teaching and learning, they feel capable, competent, and confident. To reach their full potential, Latinx children need to have equitable access to the curriculum. One way to create access is to infuse Latinx literature in the curriculum. When I was in the classroom, I engaged my students in weekly *pláticas literarias* (literature discussions) with Latinx children's literature that contained social issues with which some of them identified. Those *pláticas literarias* helped them "transform their lived experiences into knowledge" (Freire, 1970) as they searched their lives for connections to the issues in the book. Not including material that reflects the social issues with which some Latinx children are faced (linguicism, racism) negates their existence and "denies young readers an opportunity to acknowledge, understand, come to terms with, and negotiate the issues that really affect them" (Serrato, 2009). For guidelines on carrying out *pláticas literarias*, see Chapter Five.

Linguistic Resources Language is an important resource that many Latinx students possess; their bilingual abilities help them connect with rich traditions and family. However, due to the anti-Spanish sentiment in the U.S. (see Chapter One), linguicism is rampant, and many families make the painful choice not to pass their language on to their children. Research (Crawford, 2007) suggests that most English learners lose the heritage language completely by the third generation, and in some cases the second generation. Students deserve the right to "access education in their primary language or mother tongue" (Scott, Straker, & Katz, 2009). Cummins (2001) explains that "whether we do it intentionally or inadvertently, when we destroy children's language and rupture their relationship with parents and grandparents, we are contradicting the very essence of education."

Pepita Talks Twice/Pepita habla dos veces (1995) by Ofelia Dumas Lachtman is about a bilingual girl, Pepita, who decides that she is tired of speaking twice. Pepita helps her family, community, and school with her bilingual abilities until one day she decides she is "done," and will only speak English. Pepita holds to this until the family dog, Lobo, almost gets struck by a car, and she needs all of her language skills to save the dog's life. She then recognizes the power of being bilingual.

Significance for Non-Latinx Children

When we use Latinx children's literature in our teaching, we affirm the plurality of the world (Nieto, 1992). That is one reason why it is important for all children to experience it. Latinx literature benefits children who are not Latinx by:

- exposing them to languages, cultures, and ways of life that are different from their own, which helps them see that there are many ways to be in the world.
- helping them develop an empathetic view of others.
- building cultural understanding.
- showing them that, though there may be differences in the languages and cultures, human beings have similar needs, such as happiness, safety, peace, and the need to be loved.
- opening them up to new perspectives, ideas, and ways of doing things.
- deepening their knowledge and understanding of the world through accurate representations of languages and cultures.

As the Latinx population in the United States continues to grow, Latinx literature helps non-Latinx children develop a consciousness and familiarity with an important part of the U.S. population.

Reading aloud *We've Got the Whole World in Our Hands* by Rafael López

The Danger of a Singular Latinx Narrative

In her 2009 TED Talk, Chimamanda Ngozi Adichie speaks of the danger of having a singular narrative of a particular group. She shares an example from her life about when she came to the United States from Nigeria to attend college. Her roommate was surprised when she found out Adichie spoke English and shared with her a Mariah Carey tape instead of "tribal music." Her roommate had subscribed to a singular narrative of African people, which, according to Adichie, "creates stereotypes, and the problem with stereotypes is not that they are untrue, but that they are incomplete. They make one story become the only story."

Each Latinx ethnic group carries its own cultural nuances, traditions, language variations, history, ways of interacting with the environment, and ways of identifying.

While most Latinx people in the United States are of Mexican origin (Pew Hispanic Center, 2017), there is a widespread misconception that if one is Latinx, he or she is Mexican. As discussed in Chapter One, each Latinx ethnic group carries its own cultural nuances, traditions, language variations, history, ways of interacting with the environment, and ways of identifying. Viewing Latinx people as monocultural and homogenous can lead to generalizations and stereotypes.

Who Is Telling Our Cuentos?

The Cooperative Children's Book Center (CCBC) at the School of Education at the University of Wisconsin—Madison is a research library that maintains a database of books published annually for children and young adults in the United States. In 1985, it reported that only 18 of the 2,500 trade books published were written by African Americans. A decade later, the center, while continuing to collect data on books by African Americans, began collecting data on books by other groups, including American Indians/First Nations, Asian Pacifics/Asian Pacific Americans, and Latinx people.

The charts on the next page, which capture the most recent data available from the CCBC, clearly demonstrate that, although the number of books by and about people of color is increasing in the U.S., our *cuentos* are being told by others. There are more books published annually written *about* people of color (POC) than written *by* people of color.

2018–2019

Year	Books Received	Black/ African		Indigenous		Asian		Pacific Islanders		Arab		Latinx	
		By	About	By	About	By	About	By	About	By	About	By	About
2019	3,717	224	451	29	43	381	328	5	5	17	32	228	235
2018	3,335	204	388	26	34	350	309	2	6	15	24	194	243

2015–2017

Year	Books Received	African/African Americans		American Indians/ First Nations		Asian Pacifics/Asian Pacific Americans		Latinx	
		By	About	By	About	By	About	By	About
2017	3,500	126	334	18	44	260	286	109	205
2016	3,200	92	267	8	35	195	225	95	157
2015	3,200	106	244	9	28	156	107	56	79

Data on books by and about Black, Indigenous and People of Color published for children and teens compiled by the Cooperative Children's Book Center, School of Education, University of Wisconsin–Madison

Maya González, author, activist, artist, and educator, and Matthew SG, her partner at Reflection Press (reflectionpress.com/), spearheaded a movement called Children's Books as a Radical Act to raise awareness of the potential of children's books to serve as tools for social change. They believe that "children's books offer the potential to engage all of our creative faculties to transform the stories we, as people of color, queer, or indigenous people, heard as children that often did not include us" (reflectionpress.com/childrens-books-radicalact).

As educators, it us our responsibility to ensure that all children are seeing themselves represented in our classrooms, curriculum, and libraries.

Concluding Thought

While Latinx children's literature has grown in popularity since the 1990s, the number of books by Latinx authors remains relatively small. We need to continue encouraging publishers to seek out and support Latinx authors. We also need to urge school librarians to add Latinx children's literature to their collections. After all, Latinx literature is not just for Latinx children.

Indeed, our stories are treasures and gifts to be shared with *todos*. At the beginning of this chapter, Miguel showed us the excitement of seeing one's own language, culture, and community in a book. Shouldn't all children have the opportunity to experience this? Yuyi Morales (2019) eloquently explains why Latinx children's literature is for all:

> Non-Latinx children, the ones not yet familiar with the culture, open the book and encounter surprises, those that we, like all other ethnic groups, have to offer from the most precious gifts of our culture. And how could we, Latinxs, not share our legacy with others? After all, our treasures are so splendid.

Chapter Three

¿De quién son los cuentos?/ Whose Stories?

Cultural Authenticity and Selection Criteria

During my weekly visit to Tammy Frierson's preK classroom, as I made my way to the circle of children, I could tell they were excited by the questions they were asking me:

"Sra. Julia, what books do you have today?"

"What's in your bag?"

I sat in a chair and told them that I had a new book, one that I thought they would enjoy because it was by an author whose books we had read. "What is

it?" a few children asked at once. I opened my orange book bag and took out *Niño Wrestles the World* by Yuyi Morales (2013), the story of a little boy who loves to *luchar* (wrestle). In the story, he meets and defeats many *luchadores* (wrestlers) in lively, skillful ways. The vibrant comic-book-like illustrations capture the reader almost immediately. Despite that, to be honest, when I first read the book, I wasn't crazy about it. I am not sure if it was because the illustrations are so different from those in other Morales books or because I didn't connect personally to the story line, not being much of a wrestling fan. But after reading it with a group of three- to five-year-olds, I was sold!

I began the read-aloud by showing the children the back cover and then the front cover and asking them to tell me what they thought the book would be about. "A little boy because *niño* is 'boy,'" a child called out. "A boy and some monsters," another child added. "A boy in his underwear!" another squealed, which released a lot of new responses:

"Ewww! Ewwww!"

"He's in his underwear!"

"That is so gross!"

"Why is he in his underwear? Did he forget his pants? Ewww!"

It might have appeared that I had lost control because the children were talking all at once and crawling toward me to get a better look at the book. Even Mrs. Frierson, the teacher, looked perplexed by the book. In an attempt to settle the children, I asked if anyone played sports or had siblings who played sports. They called out T-ball, basketball, cheerleading, dance, and karate. I then asked what they wore when engaging in those activities. The children shared that they wore uniforms because "you can't wear what you want. There are rules."

I asked if anyone knew the meaning of *lucha libre* (wrestling) and then asked if anyone watched wrestling. Many of the children said yes, on TV. I asked them what the wrestlers wear, to which they responded a uniform and boots. I wanted the children to connect the uniforms they wore for extracurricular activities to what Niño was wearing—not only underwear, but a mask and boots. And they did just that. I also wanted the children to understand that Niño was using his imagination to play, and he was pretending to wear a *lucha libre* wrestling uniform. "We play dress up, too!" someone happily shouted. On we read. I spent about two minutes on each page because the children were so excited! When I finished, they immediately asked me to read it again. So, I did—and then one more time. I read that book three times in one sitting to a classroom of three-, four-, and five-year-old children!

What excited them so much about the book? It was interesting and relevant to them. They connected with it because some were wrestling fans and they related to a young child engaged in imaginary play with familiar toys. We talked during and after the read-aloud. The children simply could not get enough of Niño because his story helped them "generate authentic and meaningful connections" (Huerta & Tafolla, 2016). I read the book three times, and I probably could have read it three more times because the children were that enthralled by it. I returned the following week without the book, and it was a mistake. The children were so disappointed. So now I never remove *Niño Wrestles the World* from my orange book bag. Also in the bag were *Diez Deditos and Other Play Rhymes and Action Songs from Latin America*

When I visit Tammy Frierson's classroom each week, the children are always curious to learn what books I'm carrying in my orange bag.

(2002), *Fiestas: A Year of Latin American Songs of Celebration* (2002), and *De Colores and Other Latin American Folk Songs for Children* (1999), which I used as a bilingual classroom teacher years before.

My siblings and I grew into great storytellers under the influence of Papi's *cuentos*. That's me in the sunglasses!

That read-aloud taught us all about *lucha libre* and me to not judge a book by its cover. It also helped the children see that there are books about places, toys, people, and languages that are familiar to them. In other words, books with which they can connect.

Stories/*cuentos* were everywhere when I was growing up. In fact, I was raised by a storyteller. My father loved to tell *cuentos* to my siblings and me. He told *cuentos* about his life in Cuba and the joys of living in his new home, the United States, as well as his hardships as a non-English-speaking immigrant. He made the ordinary seem extraordinary by wholeheartedly investing in his storytelling. The *cuentos* he shared were funny, grand, and at times mesmerizing. They not only served as entertainment, but also reality checks about life in Cuba under a dictator and in the United States as an immigrant. Storytelling was a mode of communication (Guerra, 1998) for my father. There was always something to learn from his *cuentos*.

The Power of Story

Sonia Nieto (1997) believes that "we all have stories to tell, no matter what language they are in or what experiences they recount." Most people raised and educated in the United States would describe stories as having a beginning, middle, and end. They have a plot made up of rising action, a climax, and a resolution. But stories are so much more than that. For some cultures they *are* the culture.

A story is never simply a person's objective recounting of an event. It is a person's interpretation of an event, and the telling of it is influenced by the teller, how she views the world, and how she wants the world to see her and/or her culture. Chris Liska Carger (2005) believes that "stories are the most time-honored way in which cultures preserve the past and shape the future," while Nel Noddings (1991) suggests that "stories have the power to direct and change our lives." People tell stories all the time to share something that happened, to illustrate a point, and basically to connect with others.

Stories allow us to share our histories with the world. Through them, families convey their ways of life and their ways of being so they are not lost to future generations.

Stories, as explained by Kathy Carter (1993), are culturally bound: "In constructing stories, regardless of how convoluted and obscure they may be in particular instances, authors attempt to convey their intentions by selecting incidents and details, arranging time and sequence, and employing a variety of codes and conventions that exist in a culture." Everyone, regardless of age or socioeconomic, cultural, and linguistic background, tells stories. As Ursula K. Le Guin writes, "There have been great societies that did not use the wheel, but there have been no societies that did not tell stories" (Spooner, 2003).

Reading *Niño Wrestles the World* to a mothers' group

Because I was raised by a storyteller, one could say that I have storytelling "in my blood," and I do love to tell stories! When I was a bilingual classroom teacher, stories were a huge part of my curriculum, written stories captured in books and oral stories told by children and/or families. I read aloud several times a day to my students. I loved listening to their stories about their weekends, their birthday parties, and their journeys, such as the time they "visited their *abuelitos* at the *rancho*." My students' families often came to the classroom after school and shared their *cuentos* with me, life stories, funny stories, and stories of everyday happenings. Those stories became a regular part of our everyday conversations, which usually took place on the bench outside my classroom. The stories allowed me to learn so much about my families and them to learn so much about me, suggesting, as Paley (1990) wrote, "None of us are to be found in sets of tasks or lists of attributes; we can be known only in the unfolding of our unique stories within the context of everyday events." Furthermore, telling and carefully listening to stories leads to mutual respect and *confianza* (Gonzalez, Moll, & Amanti, 2006), which are so important in building trusting relationships with children and their families, particularly families who have been traditionally marginalized in schools.

Stories were like breathing for me, a regular part of everyday life, and nothing out of the ordinary. I saw them as recreational—as something for pure enjoyment. When my students began telling stories to make sense of the books we were reading, they made connections to their life experiences, to other books we read, and to stories their families told. They were using stories as tools to connect to and make meaning from the complex ideas we were reading about. Stories help children connect home and school, connect real-life experiences to those in books, and to see that they are a part of a world that is larger than their immediate one. They help children make sense of their lives.

Connecting Home and School Through Stories

As a teacher at Wyman School in Tucson, I was required to conduct home visits (Moll, Amanti, & González, 1992). My first "official" visit was to the home of Lorenzo Luna (pseudonym) and his father, mother, and younger sister. Prior to moving to Tucson, my knowledge of the issues related to the U.S.-Mexican border was almost nonexistent. I had moved there from Boston, which, of course, was far removed from the border both geographically and culturally. While both my parents were immigrants and struggled as most non-English-speaking immigrants of color do, their situation was quite different from the Luna family's. From Lorenzo's parents, I learned firsthand about the hardships some families face when coming to the United States.

When my students began telling stories to make sense of the books we were reading, they made connections to their life experiences, to other books we read, and to stories their families told.

The Luna family left their village in central México on an approximately six-week journey through northern Mexico's Sonoran Desert and into the United States. If it had not been for the aide and generosity of strangers, the family may not have made it through the punishing heat of the desert. Lorenzo was four years old and, according to his mother, seemed to understand the significance of their move. He was helpful and kept an eye on his one-year-old sister while his parents worked to secure their safe entry into the United States.

As Sra. Luna shared stories about the journey, much to my surprise, Lorenzo actively participated, which he didn't do at school. He was typically timid and reserved. That visit made visible the importance of connecting home and school and gave me a tangible way to do so: by sharing stories.

Connecting to the World Outside the Home Through Stories

Visiting the Luna family also fueled my interest in helping Latinx children see themselves in literature. I recognized that telling stories about his life not only gave Lorenzo the confidence to speak, but also, and equally significant, it provided him with a way to connect with the world. Because my other students and their families may also have been dealing with issues related to being new to the United States and learning English, Lorenzo helped me see the need and importance of sharing their life stories and seeing stories like theirs in books. My students needed to see that their situations and experiences were not unique to them. Although, like anyone, they had their own personal challenges, and they needed to see that they were not alone. There were others in the world who shared similar situations and experiences. Reading books and sharing stories that related to their situations and experiences would help them make sense of their lives. They would help them build a positive sense of self and provide them with a sense of belonging. I needed to provide my students with a curriculum built upon the knowledge they brought to school and that offered them time to think about and make connections among their life experiences, life stories, and school. For my students to make those connections, I engaged them in critical pedagogy and critical literacy.

Critical Pedagogy and Critical Literacy

Sonia Nieto (1999) explains that, through the lens of critical pedagogy, "teachers and students engage in learning as a mutual encounter with the world." Students actively engage in instruction in what Paulo Freire (1970) referred to as problem-posing education; they are contributors to their education rather than passive observers who "regurgitate and passively accept knowledge they are handed." Critical pedagogy is built upon students' lives, experiences, and ways of knowing. Teachers who practice it put students at the center of education by drawing from their knowledge of language, culture, and community, and place student voice in a prominent role.

Ira Shor (1999) explains that critical literacy "is language use that questions the social construction of the self. When we are critically literate, we examine our ongoing development to reveal the subjective positions from which we make sense of the world and act in it." Through engagements with text, children are taught to notice, for example, whose voices are missing and/or marginalized, who is telling the story, and if there is an implied message. They are also taught to recognize their own positions as they read and react to text. In my classroom, reading and later talking about texts during literature circles (Short, 1997), or *pláticas literarias* (López-Robertson, 2004), allowed my students to "go beneath surface meaning to understand the deep meaning" (Shor, 1992) of issues that related to them and the community.

For *pláticas literarias*, small groups of children gather to discuss books that they have read or have been read to them. The discussions are authentic, meaning they are about topics of interest to students and support Ira Shor's (1999) notion that "children are born language-users, naturally and eagerly talking about the things they do and are interested in." The *pláticas* provided my students a space to engage in "explicit discussions about their experiences" (Bartolomé, 2003) where they could think deeply about the socio-political realities of their lives (e.g., racism, poverty, and immigration) and try to make sense of them by sharing their *cuentos*.

In Chapter Four, I discuss *pláticas literaria* in detail, but here is a brief example. During a discussion of Pat Mora's *Tomás and the Library Lady*, the children were surprised that Tomás and his siblings looked for toys and books at the dump. They shared stories of going to the dump to dispose of yard brush and debris, but not to find toys and books. A few days after reading and discussing the book, one student suggested that our class should "do something to help poor children like Tomás get toys that are not from the dump." In follow-up *pláticas*, the children talked about poverty and issues related to it and presented ideas for helping children in their community in need.

Through thoughtful follow-up engagements with the text, my students recognized poverty as an important issue to tackle and took action to help those living in it. Mary Esther Huerta and Carmen Tafolla (2016) remind us that "children also need an emotional interaction with literary works that generate a point at which personal and emotional awareness permeates students' intellectual activities." That is particularly important for our Latinx children who are often not represented in the curriculum. These *pláticas* gave my students a chance to read quality literature and share their life *cuentos*, which connected them to one another and to the world beyond our classroom.

Selecting Quality Latinx Literature: ¿Cómo se hace?

Picture books capture the cultural, political, historical, and social context of the time in which they are published. At the same time, they demonstrate the worldview and attitudes of the authors and illustrators who created them. Bradford (2007) reminds us that "the language of children's books performs and embodies ideologies of all kinds" and, depending on those ideologies, the books may "affirm prejudice and the status quo" (Kim & Short, 2019). As such, it is imperative that teachers and students alike "develop the tools to critique [literature] and the printed word in general" (Nieto, 1997). They should not simply accept what they read as true.

Because we do not want to perpetuate stereotypical and sometimes harmful and inaccurate views of Latinx people, we need to use care when choosing books. Martínez-Roldán (2013) believes that "it is crucial to continue developing language for examining stereotypical representations of characters and cultures in children's books." That can be done by teaching children to carefully examine texts. You might consider hosting workshops where families can also carefully examine texts. Well-meaning families looking for diverse children's reading materials may mistakenly select books that seem appropriate, when in reality they are "embedded in a privileged dominant discourse" (Kim & Short, 2019) and present "distorted or comical representations" (Harris, 1997), which can lead to Latinx children developing an "understanding that they have little value in society in general and in school in particular" (Harris, 1997).

Because we do not want to perpetuate stereotypical and sometimes harmful and inaccurate views of Latinx people, we need to use care when choosing books.

The Skippyjon Jones (2003) book series by Judy Schachner features a Siamese cat that does not resemble his mother or sisters. Skippyjon Jones's oversized head and ears, small body, and short tail convince him that he is a Chihuahua. In a detailed analysis of *Skippyjon Jones in the Doghouse* (2005), Carmen M. Martínez-Roldán (2013) found that the book is replete with misrepresentations, stereotypes, distorted reflections of Mexican culture, and the use of mock Spanish.

Like Martínez-Roldán, I do not wish to censor the book. I do believe that Skippyjon Jones serves a few purposes. It can be used as a concrete example of books that are commercially successful while culturally inappropriate and can also be used in classrooms for careful examination of culturally insensitive and biased children's books.

The National Council of Teachers of English's position statement on People of Color (POC) in books recognizes the important role that school materials and curricula play and notes that they "should foster the development of attitudes grounded in respect for and understanding of the diverse cultures of American society" (NCTE, 2020). Presenting books that do not do that are harmful to both Latinx and non-Latinx students.

How then can teachers and families make informed book choices, especially if they are not Latinx or know enough about Latinx cultures? Indeed, according to the National Center for Education Statistics, NCES, 80 percent of public-school teachers are white females, while 49 percent of students are children of color.

Children have the right to see themselves respectfully and accurately represented in the books and curriculum. But what exactly does "respectfully and accurately represented" mean? How do we know when a book is presenting a single story? How do we choose culturally authentic books?

What is meant by cultural authenticity? You may wonder about the necessity of Latinx literature in your classroom, particularly if you do not have Latinx students. As I discussed in Chapter Two, Latinx children's literature is for all children. In the sections that follow, I discuss cultural authenticity, as well as criteria for selecting Latinx children's literature.

Aurelia reading a book she and her classmates authored

Cultural Authenticity

Debates over a definition of cultural authenticity in children's literature have been going on for some time and continue to this day (c.f. Short & Fox, 2003; Clark, Flores, Smith, & González, 2016). Mo and Shen (2003) call it a "multidimensional issue." Some believe that cultural authenticity can be achieved only when the insider (i.e., a member of the cultural group) writes the text because the outsider does not have the knowledge or dispositions to do so in an appropriate manner. Others, however, believe that allowing only certain authors to write certain stories "restricts an author's freedom to write." Kathy Short and Dana Fox (2003) suggest that the "debates about cultural authenticity in children's literature matter because they foster the dialogue that is essential to democracy and to the struggle for social justice."

Rudine Sims Bishop (2003) believes that authenticity is achieved when writers are able to "reflect the cultural perspectives" of the people they are writing about and make insiders believe that they have the inside scoop. Referring to Puerto Rican literature, Sonia Nieto (1997) offers that outsiders can write Puerto Rican literature, but they need to make sure they "capture the mood and texture of the lives of Puerto Ricans in realistic and believable ways." Finally, Lynn Atkinson Smolen and Ruth A. Oswald (2011) note that authentic literature reflects cultural groups as they exist in contemporary society, not as relics of the past. They go on to say that the "distinctive characteristics of each group are represented, avoiding the merging of subcultural groups into one group." When it comes to Latinx literature, there is no one Latinx culture. The most resonant explanation of authentic literature, in my opinion, comes from Nieto (1997):

> The search for authentic literature is not the search for an upbeat, consistently positive, sentimental, romanticized, or idealized reality. Rather, it is the search for a more balanced, complete, accurate, and realistic literature that asks even young readers to grapple with sometimes thorny issues...literature that attempts to reflect the range of issues and possibilities with the community's experience.

"The search for authentic literature is...the search for a more balanced, complete, accurate, and realistic literature that asks even young readers to grapple with sometimes thorny issues."

—Sonia Nieto

What is most important, of course, is making sure the uniqueness of the various Latinx cultures (e.g., Mexicans, Puerto Ricans, etc.) is represented accurately, respectfully, and believably.

We must ask ourselves: Who has the right to write stories about Latinx people? This issue is complicated by the statistics pointing to the low numbers of books written by Latinx authors. As noted in Chapter Two, the CCBC collects data on the number of books published in the United States. In 2018, of the 3,312 books published in the United States, 186 were written by Latinx authors while 240 were written about the Latinx communities by outsiders. While having quality Latinx literature available and accessible for children is of utmost importance, authors of color continue to be marginalized.

Choosing Culturally Authentic Books

So how do we know if a book is authentic? In 2007, Jamie Naidoo and I interviewed bilingual book publishers of and experts in Latinx children's literature to gain a better understanding of issues in writing, illustrating, and publishing bilingual books. From our research, we concluded that cultural authenticity in Latinx literature is a fusion of elements that we called *el sabor* or "flavor." Consider the following guiding questions when determining whether a piece of literature carries *el sabor*:

- Does the story come alive and carry the nuances of the culture?
- Does it help you to better understand your own culture?
- Can you identify with the book and its themes?
- Does it help you to better understand a culture different from your own and teach you something about that culture?

Worlds of Words: Center of Global Literacies and Literatures at the University of Arizona offers questions to consider when analyzing texts for cultural authenticity, which serve as a starting point for inquiry and close reading for you and your students. (See questions on the following two pages.) Together with the issues raised above regarding cultural authenticity, you may also want to share these questions with families that are interested in choosing culturally authentic books for reading at home.

Questions to Consider When Analyzing Texts for Cultural Authenticity

Literary Qualities

- How well does the author tell the story? Is it quality literature?

Origin of Book

- What is the origin of the book?
- Who was the original publisher, and in what country is it located?
- Who is the author? Illustrator? Translator? What are their backgrounds?

Authorship

- How do the author's experiences relate to the setting and characters in this book?
- On what experiences and/or research is the book based?
- Why might the author have chosen this story to tell?

Believability

- Is this story believable? Could it have happened?
- In what ways does it feel real/authentic?
- Are the characters larger than stereotypes but less than "perfect" heroes?

Accuracy of Details and Authenticity of Values

- Are there inaccurate details in the book?
- What values are at the heart of the book?
- How do those values connect to the lives of actual people within the culture?
- Does this book reflect a specific cultural experience, or could the story have happened anywhere?

Questions to Consider When Analyzing Texts for Cultural Authenticity *continued*

Perspectives and Experiences

- Whose perspectives and experiences are portrayed?
- Who tells the story?
- What is the range of insider perspectives?

Power Relationships

- Which characters have power or significance in the book?
- Who takes action?
- How is the story resolved?
- Where does the story go, and how does it get there? Who takes it there? Why?

Audience

- Who is the book's intended audience?
- Is the book written for children from a particular country or culture, or to inform children in other parts of the world about that country or culture?

Relationship to Other Books

- How does this book connect with other books about this culture?
- Do the available books about this culture capture a range of perspectives and experiences within that culture?

Response by Insiders

- How have insiders responded to this book?

Connections for Readers

- What are the possible connections for students? Is the book accessible?

Adapted by Worlds of Words in 2020 from "10 Quick Ways to Analyze Children's Books for Racism and Sexism," originally published in 1980 as a brochure by the Council on Interracial Books for Children (New York). Courtesy of Worlds of Words, The University of Arizona.

Selection Criteria

When considering Latinx children's literature, make sure it accurately and sensitively represents the culture to avoid propagating stereotypes and a singular narrative about Latinx people (e.g., they are lazy, do not speak English, and do not care about their children's education). No one story can ever tell the whole story of any culture because culture is ever-changing and dynamic. And there is not one story of any culture. So be very suspicious of any book that claims to tell the story of a particular culture, because every culture has many stories. Themes and topics may recur within and among stories, but there is no one story. Here are criteria to follow when selecting Latinx literature.

REPRESENTATION OF CULTURE

- There is not *one* Latinx culture. Does the book depict just *one* image of *all* Latinx people?

USE OF SPANISH LANGUAGE

- Is there overall respect for the Spanish language?
- Does the book contain fake Spanish or mock Spanish, such as words ending in the letter *o* to suggest Spanish?
- Does the book contain consistent and correct use of written and conversational Spanish?
- Does Spanish dialogue flow naturally, and is it free of errors?

CHARACTERS THAT ARE MULTIDIMENSIONAL

- Are the Latinx characters unnecessarily loud or boisterous?
- Are they working only in stereotypical roles, such as housekeepers, construction workers, or waitstaff?
- Are any depicted as professionals?
- Are they presented as subservient or passive?

KNOWLEDGE OF ENGLISH

- Do the characters know English, or not?
- When a character is learning English, are the people around him or her helpful and kind, or do they mock his or her attempts at the language?

EDUCATION LEVEL OF ADULTS

- Have the adult characters been formally schooled?
- Are they portrayed as simpleminded or ignorant?

STORY LINE

- Are books with Latinx characters only about immigration?
- Are the characters fleeing something? Are they running away? Being chased?

Special Considerations for Bilingual Books

- Are bilingual books, according to Schon, "faithful to the spirit, rhythm, and symmetry of both languages, and books that reflect linguistic differences, colloquialisms, and other popular expressions that add charm to the work"? (2004)
- Is the Spanish language used as a prop to sell a book? Are meaningless words inserted in the text?
- Is the use of Spanish "a degrading use of the language"? (Nieto, 1997)
- Is the use of Spanish redundant?
- Do the Spanish words break the flow of the story?
- Is the language natural? For example, a mother would not say, "hija, daughter."

Illustrations

Illustrations are vital because they help children make and extend meaning. According to Johnson, Mathis, and Short (2019), when children explore beautifully illustrated books, they are absorbed in a "visual culture in which images are integral to their experiences and interactions...images are central to how meaning is created in the world." So when selecting Latinx children's literature, be sure the images are not reinforcing stereotypes because, through books, children make meaning about the world and their place in it. Here are depictions to look for when considering books to share with children:

DEPICTION OF PEOPLE

- Are the Latinx characters afraid because they are being chased or followed?
- Are the characters being controlled by others?
- Are they depicted as troubled, dishonest, or deceitful?
- Are the Latinx characters dark and sinister?
- Are they presented as "fillers" and tokenized? Do they look like white people with different-colored skin?
- Are they similar in appearance to one another or do they each have a unique look?
- Are the illustrations of Latinx people cartoon-like?
- Do their clothing and accessories reinforce stereotypes (e.g., sombreros)?
- Are the characters portrayed as unwashed and/or lazy?
- Do they look tired and harried?
- Are they portrayed as criminals (e.g., as bandits or members of a gang)?
- Are the characters, particularly female characters, oversexualized?

DEPICTION OF FAMILY

- Is the family always financially strapped?
- Always led by a single parent, usually a mother?
- Always led by grandparents?
- Always large?

DEPICTION OF HOME

- Is the home always messy, dirty, or poorly maintained because of lack of income?
- Always small?
- Always overcrowded with extended family members?

DEPICTION OF NEIGHBORHOOD

- Are the Latinx characters always living in the barrio?
- In the "hood"?
- In subsidized housing or housing projects?

Checking for Bias

Worlds of Words adapted and updated *10 Quick Ways to Analyze Children's Books for Racism and Sexism* from the Council on Interracial Books for Children, originally published in 1980. Below is a summary of the list. For the complete list, go to wowlit.org.

Just as the earlier lists for checking for cultural authenticity of Latinx literature are a starting point for discussion, close reading, and analysis, the aim of this list is to arm you with the information you need to begin critical conversations with children, families, and fellow educators. Although the original list was published over 40 years ago, sadly, racism, sexism, and bias remain issues in children's literature today.

Check the Illustrations

Look for Stereotypes. A stereotype is an oversimplified generalization about a particular group, race, sex, or gender, which usually carries derogatory or inaccurate messages, and is applied to all members of a group. While you may not find stereotypes in blatant forms, look for variations that demean, ridicule, or patronize characters because of their race, sex, or gender.

Look for Active Doers. Do the illustrations depict characters of color in subservient and passive roles or in leadership and action roles? Who is depicted as needing help and who takes action? Are males the active doers and females the inactive observers? Are gender identities portrayed that go beyond a female/male binary?

Check the Story Line

Although blatant racist and sexist representations are no longer prevalent, racist and sexist attitudes and assumptions still find more subtle expression in books. Some of the subtle forms of bias include the following:

Standards for Success. Is "making it" in the dominant white society projected as the only ideal? To gain acceptance and approval, do persons of color have to exhibit extraordinary qualities—excel in sports, get As, etc.? In friendships between white children and children of color, does the child of color have to do most of the understanding and forgiving?

Resolution of Problems. How are problems presented, conceived, and resolved in the story? Are people of color considered to be "the problem"? Are the oppressions faced by people of color and women represented as related to social injustice? Are the reasons for poverty and oppression explained, or are they accepted as inevitable? Does the story line encourage passive acceptance or active resistance? Is a particular problem that is faced by a person of color resolved through the benevolent intervention of a white person? Who causes and who resolves the problem?

Role of Women. Are the achievements of girls and women based on their own initiative and intelligence, or are they due to their good looks or to their relationship with boys? Are gender roles incidental or critical to characterization and plot? Could the same story be told if the gender roles are shifted? Are there characters with a range of gender identities?

Look at the Lifestyles

Are people of color and their setting depicted in such a way that they contrast unfavorably with the unstated norm of white middle-class suburbia? If people of color are depicted as "different," are negative value judgments implied? Are people of color depicted exclusively in ghettos, barrios, or migrant camps? If the illustrations and text attempt to depict a particular culture, do they go beyond oversimplifications and offer genuine insight into the lifestyles of the characters?

Do the white people in the story possess the power, take the leadership, and make the important decisions? Do people of color and females primarily function in supporting roles?

Look for inaccuracy and inappropriateness in the depiction of cultures outside of dominant white society. Watch for instances of the "quaint-natives-in-costume" syndrome, which is most noticeable in areas like clothing and customs, but also extends to behavior and personality traits.

Weigh the Relationships Between People

Do the white people in the story possess the power, take the leadership, and make the important decisions? Do people of color and females primarily function in supporting roles?

How are family relationships depicted? In African American families, is the mother always dominant? In Latinx families, is the family always portrayed as struggling? If the family is separated, are societal conditions—unemployment, poverty, for example—cited among the reasons for the separation? Are characters from a range of genders portrayed in nurturing roles?

Children enjoying *Call Me Tree/Llámame árbol* by Maya Christina Gonzalez

Note the Heroes

For many years, books showed only "safe" heroes of color, in particular those who avoided serious conflict with the white establishment of their time. People of color today insist on the right to define their own heroes (of any gender) based on their own concepts and struggles for justice. When heroes of color do appear, are they admired for the same qualities that have made white heroes famous or because what they have done has benefited white people? Ask, "Whose interest is a particular hero really serving?"

Consider the Effect on a Child's Self-Image

Are norms established that limit any child's aspirations and self-concept? Children of color are often bombarded with images of the color white as the ultimate in beauty, cleanliness, virtue, etc., and the color black as evil, dirty, menacing, etc. Does the book counteract or reinforce this positive association with the color white and negative association with black? Will all children of color from a range of backgrounds find one or more characters with whom they can readily and positively identify? Are there gender associations based on who performs brave and important deeds? What concept of beauty is portrayed, and does that concept of beauty vary by gender?

Consider the Author or Illustrator's Background

Analyze the biographical material on the jacket flap or the back of the book. If a story deals with a theme related to a specific minoritized group, what qualifies the author or illustrator to deal with the subject? If the author or illustrator are not members of the minoritized group being written about, is there anything in their background that would recommend them as the creators of this book? Also, consider the same issues related to other members of the bookmaking team if such people are known—e.g., translator, editor, publicist.

Check Out the Author's Perspective

No author can be wholly objective. All authors write out of a cultural as well as personal context. In the past, more children's books were created by white, middle-class authors and illustrators, so that a single ethnocentric perspective dominated children's literature in the United States. Read carefully to determine whether the direction of the author's perspective substantially weakens or strengthens the value of the book. Are omissions and distortions central to the character or message of the book? Check the websites of the author and illustrator to read their statements and perspectives in discussing their creation of the book.

Watch for Loaded Words

A word is loaded when it has insulting overtones. Examples of loaded adjectives (usually racist) are *savage*, *lazy*, *conniving*, *superstitious*, *treacherous*, *wily*, *crafty*, *docile*, and *backward*.

Look for sexist and gendered language and adjectives that exclude or ridicule women or exclude gender identities beyond male/female. Look for use of the male pronoun to refer to both males and females or the use of binary language that signals that the only two options for gender identity are male or female. While the generic use of the word *man* was accepted in the past, its use today is outmoded. The following examples show how sexist language can be avoided: substitute *ancestors* for *forefathers*, *chairperson* for *chairman*, *community* for *brotherhood*, *firefighters* for *firemen*, *manufactured* for *man-made*, *the human family* instead of *the family of man*. Examples of how gendered language can be avoided include substituting *siblings* for *brother and sister*, *parents* for *mom and dad*, *children* for *boys and girls*, and *they* for *he/she*.

Look at the Copyright Date

Books with characters of color did not appear, for the most part, until the mid-1960s, many of which were published to meet the new market demand but were still written by white authors, edited by white editors, and published by white publishers. They therefore reflected a white point of view. Authors of colors writing about their own experiences emerged in the 1970s, but this trend has fluctuated with the market over the years. Non-sexist books, with rare exceptions, were not published before 1973. The copyright dates, therefore, can be a clue as to how likely the book is to be overtly racist or sexist or gendered, although a recent copyright date is no guarantee of a book's relevance or sensitivity. The copyright date only means the year the book was published. It usually takes several years from the time a manuscript is submitted to the publisher to the time it is printed. This time lag meant little in the past but is significant in a time period of rapid change and evolving consciousness as children's book publishing attempts to be relevant.

Concluding Thought

We want children to connect with texts that depict a variety of cultures, languages, and ways of being in the world. We do not want them to view people from cultures different from their own as "exotic" or "foreign." That is why book selection matters. When books are haphazardly selected, we risk reinforcing stereotypes. Selecting quality Latinx literature involves close reading and careful analysis for cultural authenticity. Presenting students, particularly Latinx students, with books that accurately and respectfully represent Latinx cultures is important because of its impact. For many years, "the low representation of Latinos in the world of books created social distance between the ethnic minority child and the educational system when the perceived distance from the world of books sustained the belief that it is not relevant to their life" (Huerta & Tafolla, 2016).

Latinx children's literature is a powerful tool to help students succeed in learning and life. It also helps to build community in the classroom and the school. When students are exposed to multicultural literature, they are less likely to find themselves feeling invisible and, instead, find themselves feeling more engaged in classroom activities. Just as important, if you use literature that transcends simple stereotypes, all students develop a sense of respect and understanding for one another. Choose books that are authentic and create a connection between the authors and the readers (Guevara, 2003) so that children develop the habit of eagerly asking, "What books do you have today?!"

Chapter Four

¿Y ahora qué?/Now What?

Using Latinx Children's Literature in the Classroom

Although I am no longer a classroom teacher, I spend a lot of time with young children in classrooms doing what I love: reading to and with them, especially Latinx children's books and stories, and singing songs. It all began when my youngest child, Pedro, began preschool, a Montessori program at a preK–5 school. A few weeks after school began, I asked his teacher if I could come in and share books and songs in Spanish with

the children, to which she immediately and very happily answered "yes!" For the next seven years, I would spend about an hour every Friday in the classroom reading, singing, doing fingerplays, and playing games with the 20 African American, Indian, and white children. Pedro was the only Latinx child. I brought in multicultural literature that represented the children in the classroom, as well as English/Spanish bilingual books and books completely in Spanish to share with the class.

Playing "Un elefante se balanceaba" from *De Colores and Other Latin American Folksongs for Children*

Of all the beautiful memories that I have from my seven years in that classroom, one stands out. I was reading aloud in Spanish the bilingual picture book *I Know the River Loves Me/Yo sé que el río me ama* (González, 2009), when one child called out, "I don't understand those words." Mrs. Frierson, the teacher, had always supported my methods and often participated in my read-alouds. And she did not miss a beat this time. She said to the class, "I don't understand some words either, but I am learning. I am so excited to learn a language that I don't know and just love all these stories. Let's listen and look at the pictures. I bet we can figure things out. And if we can't, our friends can help us. One of our friends knows a lot of Spanish, and I know he'll help us." The child who spoke out looked at me, the book, his one Spanish-speaking classmate, and asked, "Pedro, will you help me in Spanish?" Pedro's response: "Yes, I am bilingual and will help everyone because I can." That was it. A child expressed her concern about feeling a little lost, a teacher lovingly responded and drew on one child's linguistic gift, his bilingualism, and on we went.

In this chapter, I provide ideas and strategies for incorporating Latinx children's literature into the curriculum in meaningful, engaging ways. It is important to choose appropriate literature, as discussed in Chapter Three, and to incorporate that literature into the curriculum in a meaningful manner throughout the school year, not only at a particular time in the school year, such as Hispanic Heritage Month, or to focus on a limited range of topics such as food, folklore, fashion, famous people, and festivals (Meyer & Rhoades, 2006). When we limit the use of Latinx literature, we risk offering a single narrative of Latinx people, as discussed in Chapter Two. We risk presenting Latinx people as "exotic" and "foreign," and not part of the fabric of our society. For help in how to choose high-quality Latinx children's literature, visit scholastic.com/CuentosResources.

Recognize Language as a Gift

I want teachers to understand and appreciate the myriad ways of knowing and making meaning that students bring with them to school. At the same time, I want children and families to continue to feel proud to be Latinx and speak Spanish. Gloria Anzaldúa (2007) reminds us that "ethnic identity is twin skin to linguistic identity...until I can take pride in my language, I cannot take pride in myself." Language is a part of who we are, a gift that is given from one generation to the next (López-Robertson, 2014). One way to ensure that happens is to convey to families and children the importance of maintaining and passing along the home language. It's a good practice to read and engage all children in Latinx literature and encourage emergent bilinguals to use their language in school.

Practice Translanguaging

Remember that not all Latinx children have the gift of speaking Spanish and that this is a deliberate choice made by their families and parents. The United States has a complicated history with language rights as discussed in Chapter One, a history that continues to impact federal attitudes, policies, and procedures for children who speak languages in addition to English. Rather than adopt a language pedagogy that recognizes and builds upon their varied and dynamic language practices (Vogel & García, 2017), emergent bilinguals—students who speak two or more languages in their daily lives—are frequently

Picture Books That Invite Translanguaging

Isla (1999) by Arthur Dorros and illustrator Elisa Kleven. Using her imagination, Rosalba journeys to the Caribbean island where her abuela grew up and sees all the beauty of the island, from the capital city to the tropical rainforest.

Papá and Me (2014) by Arthur Dorros and illustrator Rudy Gutierrez. A bilingual book about the bond between a papá and his son.

Carmela Full of Wishes (2018) by Matt de la Peña and illustrator Christian Robinson. It is Carmela's birthday, and she is finally old enough to join her older brother as they run family errands. She finds a dandelion and has one wish she can make. What will she wish for?

What Can You Do with a Rebozo?/¿Qué puedes hacer con un rebozo? (2009) by Carmen Tafolla and illustrator Amy Cordova. Using your imagination there is no limit to what you can do with a *rebozo*, a traditional Mexican woven shawl.

What Can You Do with a Paleta? (2009) by Carmen Tafolla and illustrator Magaly Morales. The *paletero* makes his way through el barrio, ringing his bell to let everyone know that icy-cold fruity treats, *paletas,* have arrived.

¡A bailar!/Let's Dance (2011) by Judith Ortiz Cofer. Marita and her mother practice dancing in the kitchen as they prepare for a concert in the park where papi plays the trombone.

The Tooth Fairy Meets El Ratón Pérez (2010) by Rene Colato Laínez and illustrator Tom Lintern. The United States has the Tooth Fairy, and Latin America and Spain have El Ratón Pérez. What happens when they arrive to claim a Mexican American boy's tooth?

Querido primo: Una carta a mi primo (2017) and **Dear Primo: A Letter to My Cousin** (2018) by Duncan Tonatiuh. Two cousins, one in Mexico and the other in the United States, write letters to each other and discover how similar their lives are.

¡Vamos! Let's Go to the Market (2020) by Raúl the Third. Little Lobo and his dog, Bernabe, deliver supplies to vendors who sell a variety of items such as piñatas, carved masks, and comic books.

¡Vamos! Let's Go Eat (2020) by Raúl the Third. To help his friends prepare for a wrestling show, Little Lobo and his dog, Bernabe, take lunch orders from the *luchadores*. We follow along as they visit various food trucks.

kept from using those practices by teachers and/or administrators who are not familiar with the research supporting bilingualism and multilingualism. In *Rooted in Strength*, Cecilia Espinosa and Laura Ascenzi-Moreno (2021) demonstrate how our emergent bilinguals thrive when they are able to use "translanguaging" to tap the power of their entire linguistic and sociocultural repertoires. At the core of that approach is leveraging the language and cultural resources emergent bilinguals bring to school—and rooting instruction in their strengths. It positions emergent bilinguals as holders and creators of knowledge (Bernal, 2002).

Read Aloud ... a Lot!

A read-aloud serves many purposes. It provides an escape, taking children into unknown or unexpected places. It ignites their interests and helps them find answers to inquiries. It affirms their sense of identity and helps them take pride in who they are. Regarding books dealing with immigration, Patricia Sánchez and Maité Landa (2016) say that they provide a "type of therapy that allows [children] to understand that their experience is not something they need to fear or something of which to be ashamed." Read-alouds can also be used as instructional tools for modeling language, expressive reading, vocabulary, and fluency. They may also serve, simply, as a great source of pleasure. When I was teaching young children, I read aloud at least three times a day. That may sound like a lot, but it is not. Sometimes I read a poem or sang a song while the children followed along (usually we sang along to the CD, as I am not a singer)! I often read half of the book and left the children wondering what was going to happen next!

In fact, I began each day with a song, followed by other activities, which usually involved some writing: a greeting, the calendar, lunch count, the math problem of the day. That was followed by our language arts block, which I kicked off with a read-aloud related to our unit of study. In addition to reading the book, I used it to prompt thinking, pose questions, provide information, and/or point out something about language (e.g., exclamation point use, the author's craft move).

After lunch and recess, most of the children were tired from all the running and playing they did. So, I read aloud a picture book or chapter book to help them refocus and sometimes allowed them a quick nap! I read picture books in their entirety and a chapter or a few paragraphs from chapter books.

I ended the day with a poem or song and sometimes with another read-aloud. Often, I would read only a few pages of a book to leave the children wondering what was going to happen next, which was a great way to start the following school day. They loved these cliff-hangers! The children arrived to class excited to finish the book! I ended each read-aloud with a rhyme: "*Colorín colorado*," and my students would respond, "*Este cuento se ha acabado*." which basically translates to, "The story has ended," but in a lyrical way.

Interactive Read-Aloud

In an interactive read-aloud, you periodically stop reading and engage the children in conversation about the book. To prepare, read the book and select stopping points, depending on the strategy you are teaching. While you read aloud, ask the children to listen actively and think about the text, and then have them engage in partner or small-group conversations about the book.

Recently, I read aloud *Evelyn Del Rey Is Moving Away* (2020) by Meg Medina. Here's a summary: Evelyn and Daniela are best friends who live across the street from each other and do everything together, until it is time for Evelyn to move away.

I showed the book to the children and asked them what they thought the book was about. I said, "I think that one of the girls is moving. I can see the boxes in the truck. Please turn to the person next to you and tell him or her what you predict the book is about." After a few minutes, I called them together and began reading, pausing at my preselected spots.

In the chart below, I offer some strategies you can teach and model during the interactive read-aloud, which may also serve as sentence starters when children write a response to a read-aloud.

Strategies to Teach and Model During Interactive Read-Aloud

CONNECTING	RESPONSE	CLARIFYING
I am thinking…	I feel…	I am not sure of…
I am noticing…	My favorite part is…	I was confused by…
I understand…	I like…	
I am feeling…	I am for…	
I am figuring out…	I dislike…	
I just learned that…	I am against…	
	I agree…	
	I disagree…	
	My opinion is…	

REFLECTING	QUESTIONING	PREDICTING
I wonder why…	I think this is…	I predict…
I enjoyed…	I know that …	I think this is…
I can't believe…	My guess is…	I know that …
I disliked…		My guess is…
I liked…		

SUMMARY	VISUALIZING	SYNTHESIZING
The main idea is…	I see…	Now I feel that…
The story is mostly about…	I picture…	

You can download this chart at scholastic.com/CuentosResources.

Drama Inspired by Read-Alouds

After reading aloud *Niño Wrestles the World* (Morales, 2015) several times, Tammy Frierson and I engaged the children in recreating the story through

drama. At Yuyi Morales's website (yuyimorales. com/2.htm) we found masks of the various characters. We printed out the masks and asked the children to choose which character they would like to be. Of course, everyone said, "Niño!" And we explained that not everyone could be the same character. Nonetheless, we ended up with a few more Niños than we had planned for, but it was fine. Over the next few days, the children colored the masks, rehearsed their lines, and at the end of the week put on the play. They were all so engaged and had a lot of fun!

Children in their *Niño Wrestles the World* masks

Create Class Books Inspired by Existing Texts

A fun way to engage readers is by creating class books inspired by favorite read-alouds. *Listen to the Desert/Oye al desierto* (Mora, 1994) is a lyrical

bilingual story about the sounds of nature in the desert. When I read it to my first graders, I called their attention to those sounds: for example, "Listen to the snake hiss, tst-tst-tst. tst-tst-tst." I asked the children if there are other ways to describe the sounds of a snake. Sandra said, "Listen to the snake slither, slither, slither." While saying *slither*, she stretched out her arms and wiggled them as if they were slithering like snakes. Recognizing that the book repeats each sound three times, Sandra did the same: "slither, slither, slither."

We decided to write a class book inspired by *Listen to the Desert/Oye al desierto*. After talking about many possible locations to focus on, we chose the school playground. We started writing by making a list of the items we would include: the slide, the climbing bars, the sandboxes, the ants, thunder, children, and our class pet, Iggy, an iguana who starred in many of our stories. We then made a list of the sounds for each item. From there, we wrote the book, *Oye al patio/Listen to the Playground*, in Spanish and English. Here is a sample:

Oye la Iggy, pat, pat, pat.
Oye la Iggy, pat, pat, pat.
Listen to the slide, swish, swish, swish.
Listen to the slide, swish, swish, swish.
Oye los truenos, ¡BOOM, BOOM, BOOM!
Oye los truenos, ¡BOOM, BOOM, BOOM!

While *Listen to the Desert/Oye al desierto* contained bilingual text on each page, our book alternated in Spanish and English, page by page. We had talked about the choices authors make, and that was a choice the children made as authors. When we read it together, not only did we make the sounds, but we added movement. This well-loved book was housed in our classroom library along with other books we had made. By the year's end I had repaired it with so much tape that it looked laminated!

Rocío, a preK teacher, read *The Empanadas That Abuela Made/Las empanadas que hacía la abuela* (2003) by Diane Bertrand to her preK class and, after talking about it, asked the children to think about any connections they made. Each child then made his or her own book based on the picture book.

Miguelito drew the picture and then dictated in Spanish as Rocío wrote the title of the book, *Mi mami me hace empanadas*/My Mommy Makes Me Empanadas. The page of his book reads, *Me estoy comiendo el chocolate. Y después me como la empanada, y voy a comer papas y queso.*

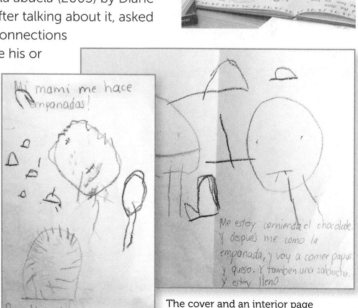

The cover and an interior page from Miguelito's book

Y también una salchicha. Y estoy lleno./I am eating chocolate. And then I eat the empanada and potatoes and cheese. And also, a sausage. And I am full.

Write Language Experience Stories

Language experience stories are stories about children's lives; these can be written independently about personal experiences or as a class about a shared experience. As a teacher, I loved taking my students on field experiences; some places we visited were the Botanical Gardens, Children's Museum, the public library, and the University of Arizona. Each of my students was paired with a preservice teacher at the University of Arizona with whom they exchanged weekly pen pal letters throughout the semester! Our last pen pal letter was delivered in person as my students, some families, and I made our way to campus.

Javier's page in our class book

We wrote books about our field trips. At left is a page written in Spanish by Javier that says that he would like a pen pal because the pen pal would read with him and help him with words in the book. Other books were about things we did in school. Together, we would map out our book: beginning, middle, and end, just like when they wrote individual stories.

How Iggy the iguana takes a bath, according to my first graders

Depending on the kind of book we decided to write, each child would work on a part of the story individually or partner up with someone. We had a class pet, an iguana named Iggy, that was about four feet long and weighed more than some of my first graders. Toward the end of each school year, the class would write a book letting the incoming first graders know about Iggy and how to take care of her. The picture answers the question, How does Iggy take a bath? We warm up the water in the microwave, put her in the sink, and scrub her and file her nails.

As I noted earlier, I spend time weekly in classrooms reading and singing with children. As an end-of-the-year gift, Mrs. Frierson's class made a bilingual book for me entitled *Queen Dr. López-Robertson/Reina Dra. López-Robertson*, which was about our weekly reading adventures and written in the form of a fairytale. It began, "There once was a far-off land called Freedomville where everyone lived safe and happily under the rule of Queen Dr. López-Robertson. She had three rules in her kingdom." I escaped the guards at the castle (i.e., the university) to go see the children each week. While at school, I read and sang with the children and then "bid them farewell and slipped back into the castle." At the castle, "she would dream of her next visit and all the books and songs she would share with the town's children."

This bilingual class book was created as a gift for me. The children titled it *Queen Dr. López-Robertson/Reina Dra. López-Robertson.*

interior pages

Take Full Advantage of the Classroom Library

Literature takes children to places they may not know exist. It enables them to travel "outside the boundaries of their lives to other places, times, and ways of living to participate in alternative ways of being in the world" (Short, 2016). As discussed throughout this book, the books in our schools and classrooms should reflect our students' lives *and* expose them to diverse cultures, languages, and ways of being.

Exposure to a wide variety of books also sparks children's curiosity and builds their awareness of the global nature of our world. School and classroom libraries play a significant role in children's reading lives, and subsequently their development as strong readers and thinkers (Miller & Sharp, 2018).

The school library is vital not only to the development of children's reading, but also to the development of reading cultures within the building. That said, a purposefully organized classroom library allows you to provide more targeted support to meet children's needs and interests (Miller & Sharp, 2018). Because you know those needs and interests probably better than anyone, you're in the best position to choose library materials that will expand students' interests and create new ones. It's also important to stock your classroom library with books to use in lessons, books that connect to content areas, mentor texts for teaching writing, and materials that invite students to think critically about social issues (López-Robertson, 2012). As noted in NCTE's Position Statement on Classroom Libraries (2017), classroom libraries "play a key role in providing access to books and promoting literacy; they have the potential to increase student motivation, engagement, and achievement and help students become critical thinkers, analytic readers, and informed citizens." While a classroom library can be packed with books depicting diverse viewpoints and representing unheard voices, that doesn't matter if the children are not engaging with those books.

Carry Out Author Studies With Children and Families

An author study provides children the opportunity to dig deeply into one author by examining his or her works and life. It helps children see an author as a real person as they learn about his or her interests and influences and examine how the author communicates meaning through pictures and words. Children of all ages can participate in author studies; the depth to which they engage will depend on grade level and interest.

I worked with a wonderful reading coach, Mary Jade Haney, at Horrell Hill Elementary School, who connected me with a group of Latinx children and their mothers. Together we engaged in an author study of Maya Christina González, focusing on three of her books: *Call Me Tree/Llámame árbol* (2014), *My Colors, My World/Mis colores, mi mundo* (2013), and *I Know the River Loves Me/Yo sé que el río me ama* (2012). All three books are bilingual, which was wonderful because it meant that the mothers whose preferred language was Spanish could access the texts.

Beloved educator Mary Jade Haney creating art during the author study

Like all of González's books, *Call Me Tree/Llámame árbol* (2014) contains bright and inviting illustrations. The book asks the reader to consider the similarities between children and trees: both are strong, vibrant, and have something to contribute to the world. *My Colors, My World/ Mis colores, mi mundo* (2013) is the story of the colors that make up a little girl's world, from her favorite hot pink to the *anaranjado* [orange] of the mud pies she makes on hot days to the red of the swings she built with her papi. Lastly, *I Know the River Loves Me/Yo sé que el río me ama* (2012) is about young Maya's favorite place, *el río*/the river. In the book, the author explores the river in different seasons— for example, swimming in the summer and watching how the river changes in the winter.

A mother and child doing artwork as part of the author study

While engaged in the author study, we visited the author's webpage (mayagonzalez.com/) and learned about her life and interests and considered how they influenced her artwork and writing. The mothers and children made many personal connections to the three books. While the children preferred *My Colors, My World/Mis colores, mi mundo*, the mothers connected to *I Know the River Loves Me/Yo sé que el río me ama*. The children talked about their favorite colors and were grossed out by the page showing young Maya in the dirt making the mud pies. I asked them, "Haven't you ever played in mud?" to which they responded, "Ewww!" until one brave child admitted that he liked squishing mud through his toes. The mothers shared personal stories of spending time with their families at rivers in their home countries—of the hours spent in the cold water on hot summer days.

Our culminating project was making a family book about the children's favorite places. They worked with their families to create bright and inviting illustrations like Maya Christina González's. After our celebration at the end of the author study, the children took the books home with them, but they shared them often with different classrooms.

Illustrator Studies

The illustrations in picture books extend the story and in many cases are works of art in and of themselves! Teaching children how to understand, appreciate, and create art like the art found in the books they read engages them in a medium different from writing and helps them see that art is also a form of communicating. Through studying the illustrations in picture books, students can engage in self-directed creation of art; engage collaboratively in creative art-making in response to an artistic problem; use observation and investigation in preparation for making a work of art; and design with various materials and tools to explore personal interests, questions, and curiosity (visual arts standards).

Many picture books have a note explaining the illustration style that was used to create the book either in front matter or at the back of the book. Additionally, many illustrators make videos where they invite readers into their studios and share the process they went through in creating their books. One of the most prolific illustrators is Yuyi Morales, whose videos are readily found on YouTube.

Favorite Latinx Children's Authors

Alma Flor Ada

almaflorada.com/ Alma Flor Ada, Professor Emerita at the University of San Francisco, has devoted her life to advocacy for peace by promoting a pedagogy oriented to personal realization and social justice. Alma Flor has written numerous children's books of poetry, narrative, folklore, and nonfiction; *The Gold Coin* (1994) , *My Name Is María Isabel* (1995), *Under the Royal Palms* (1998), and, with F. Isabel Campoy, *Yes, We Are Latinos!* (2013). In 2012, she received the Virginia Hamilton Award in recognition of her body of work for children. In 2014, the Mexican government honored her with the prestigious OHTLI Award for her services to the Mexican communities in the United States.

Monica Brown

monicabrown.net/ Monica Brown is the author of the Lola Levine chapter book series, the Sarai chapter book series, and many award-winning picture books, including *Waiting for the Biblioburro* (2011) and *Marisol McDonald Doesn't Match/Marisol McDonald no combina* (2011). Her picture book biographies include *Tito Puente: Mambo King/Tito Puente: Rey del Mambo* (2013), and *Pablo Neruda: Poet of the People* (2011). Monica's books are inspired by her Peruvian-American heritage and desire to share Latinx stories with children.

David Bowles

davidbowles.us/about/ David Bowles is a Mexican American author and translator from south Texas, where he teaches at the University of Texas Río Grande Valley. He has written several award-winning titles, most notably *The Smoking Mirror* (2015) and *They Call Me Güero* (2018). In 2019 he co-founded the hashtag and activist movement #DignidadLiteraria, which has negotiated greater Latinx representation in publishing.

Carmen Agra Deedy

carmenagradeedy.com/ Carmen Agra Deedy was born in Havana, Cuba, and came to the U.S. as a refugee in 1964. She grew up in Decatur, Georgia, and has been writing for children for over two decades. She has spoken before Noble Laureates and Pulitzer Prize winners, CEOs of major corporations, and heads of state. Over a span of 20 years, Deedy has told stories to hundreds of thousands of school children. They remain her favorite audiences. Some titles include *The Library Dragon* (2012), *Martina, the Beautiful Cockroach: A Cuban Folktale* (2013), *14 Cows for America* (2016), and *The Rooster Who Would Not Be Quiet!* (2017).

Margarita Engle

margaritaengle.com/ Margarita Engle was born in Los Angeles but developed a deep attachment to her mother's homeland, Cuba, during childhood summers with relatives on the island. She studied agronomy and botany along with creative writing, and now lives in central California with her husband. Margarita is a Cuban American author of many verse novels, memoirs, and picture books. *A Song of Frutas* (2021), *Dancing Hands: How Teresa Carreño Played the Piano for President Lincoln* (2019), *All the Way to Havana* (2017), and *Drum Dream Girl* (2015).

Maya Christina Gonzalez

mayagonzalez.com/ Maya Gonzalez is an artist, author, educator, activist, peacemaker, publisher, equality lover, obsessive recycler, traveler, river lover, tree talker, and sky kisser. Her fine art graces the cover of *Contemporary Chicano/a Art* and is well documented as part of the Chicano Art Movement. She has illustrated over 20 award-winning children's books, several of which she has also written, including Ernesto Javier Martínez's *When We Love Someone We Sing to Them/Cuando amamos cantamos* (2018), *My Colors, My World/Mis colores, mi mundo* (2013), *Call Me Tree* (2014), and *I Know the River Loves Me/Yo sé que el río me ama* (2009).

Juan Felipe Herrera

poetryfoundation.org/poets/juan-felipe-herrera Juan Felipe Herrera was born in Fowler, California. The son of migrant farmers, Herrera moved often, living in trailers or tents along the roads of the San Joaquin Valley in Southern California. As a child, he attended school in a variety of small towns from San Francisco to San Diego. In 2015, Herrera was named Poet Laureate of the United States. His books of prose for children include *Jabberwalking* (2018), *Portraits of Hispanic American Heroes* (2014), *Calling the Doves* (2001), and *Upside Down Boy* (2006).

René Colato Laínez

renecolatolainez.com/ René Colato Laínez is a graduate of the Vermont College MFA program in Writing for Children and Young Adults. He has been a bilingual elementary teacher at Fernangeles Elementary School, where he is known by the students as "the teacher full of stories." René is the author of many books for children, including *I Am René, the Boy* (2005), *Playing Lotería* (2006), *René Has Two Last Names* (2009), and *My Shoes and I: Crossing Three Borders/Mis zapatos y yo: Cruzando tres fronteras* (2019).

Juana Martínez-Neal

juanamartinezneal.com/ Juana Martinez-Neal was born in Peru, and lives in Connecticut with her family. Juana is the daughter and granddaughter of painters. She is the recipient of a Caldecott Honor, a Sibert Medal, and a Pura Belpré Medal for Illustration. Her books include *Alma and How She Got Her Name* (2019), *Fry Bread: A Native American Family Story* (2019), *Babymoon* (2019), *Swashby and the Sea* (2020), and *Zonia's Rainforest* (2021).

Meg Medina

megmedina.com/ Meg Medina is an award-winning and *New York Times* best-selling author who writes picture books, as well as middle grade and young adult fiction. When not writing, Meg works on community projects that support girls, Latinx youth, and/or literacy. Meg's works have been called "heartbreaking," "lyrical," and "must-haves for every collection." Her books include *Merci Suárez Can't Dance* (2021), *Merci Suárez Changes Gears* (2020), *Evelyn Del Rey Is Moving Away* (2020), *Mango, Abuela, and Me* (2016), and *Tía Isa Wants a Car* (2012),

Pat Mora

patmora.com/ Pat Mora is an award-winning author of books for children and adults, a literacy advocate, and a popular presenter. In 1996, she founded Children's Day, Book Day, in Spanish, El día de los niños, El día de los libros. Pat and her partners, including the American Library Association and First Book, nationally promote this yearlong initiative of creatively linking all children and families to books and establishing annual Book Day celebrations. Pat's poetry collections for children include *Bookjoy, Wordjoy* (2018); *Book Fiesta!: Celebrate Children's Day/Book Day; Celebremos El día de los niños/El día de los libros* (2016); and *Yum! ¡MmMm! ¡Qué rico!* (2007).

Yuyi Morales

yuyimorales.com/2.htm Born and raised in Mexico where she currently resides, Yuyi Morales lived for many years in the San Francisco Bay Area, where she still maintains close relations with booksellers and librarians. A professional storyteller, dancer, choreographer, puppeteer, and artist, she has won the prestigious Pura Belpré Award for Illustration six times for *Just a Minute* (2016), *Los Gatos Black on Halloween* [author Marisa Montes] (2016), *Just in Case* (2018), *Niño Wrestles the World* (2013), *Dreamers* (2018), and *Viva Frida* (2014), which also received a Caldecott Honor.

José Luis Orozco

joseluisorozco.com/ José-Luis Orozco is a bilingual educator, children's author, and recording artist who has dedicated his life to creating quality bilingual music, books, and videos for children. He encourages learning of the Spanish language and promotes Latin American culture through his art. His rich catalog includes 15 CDs, a DVD, and three award-winning songbooks: *De colores* (1994), *Rin, Rin, Rin, Do, Re, Mi* (2009), and *Fiestas* (2002).

Duncan Tonatiuh

duncantonatiuh.com/ Duncan Tonatiuh is an award-winning author-illustrator. He is both Mexican and American. He grew up in San Miguel de Allende, Mexico, and graduated from Parsons School of Design and Eugene Lang College in New York City. His artwork is inspired by Pre-Columbian art, particularly that of the Mixtec codices. His aim is to create images and stories that honor the past, but that are relevant to people, especially children, nowadays: *The Princess and the Warrior* (2016), *Funny Bones* (2015), *Separate Is Never Equal* (2014), *Pancho Rabbit and the Coyote* (2013), *Diego Rivera: His World and Ours* (2012), and *Dear Primo* (2010).

Use Text Sets

A text set is a collection of resources grouped together by theme or topic. I say "resources" because, in our work with children, we should let them know that a text is not limited to a book. A text is a poem or song, a video, a documentary, a map, a chart, a nonfiction article, a piece of art, or an informational brochure or pamphlet. Text sets allow for deep exploration of a theme or topic and allow students to explore their own curiosity about that theme or topic.

Text Set: Wrestling and *Lucha Libre*

As I shared in Chapter Three, *Niño Wrestles the World* (Morales, 2013) lives in my orange book bag that holds my treasures for classroom visits. Children have taught me that I must never be without this book! While I was reading it during my weekly visit to a multi-age classroom of three-, four-, and five-year-olds, the children asked (and answered) all sorts of questions related to wrestling and *lucha libre*: Why do they wear masks? Why do they wear underwear? Where are the girl wrestlers? Why do they fight? Their teacher later told me that the questions kept coming long after I left that day. Knowing how interested the children were in wrestling and *lucha libre*, I decided that for my next few visits I would focus on a different book on those topics. During the visits, the children and I would list questions that they wanted answered. During the read-alouds, we talked about what we noticed in the books and learned from reading them. The children also got answers to their questions.

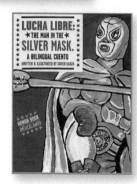

One of the longest books that I read to the children is *Lucha Libre: The Man in the Silver Mask: A Bilingual Cuento* by Xavier Garza (2005), which tells the story of Carlito's attending his first-ever *lucha libre* match in Mexico City. I was not sure that the children would sit through the book due to its length (of all the books I read, this one was more complicated), but because of their interest, they listened, talked, and examined every page of the book as I read! The next book I read, *The Great and Mighty Nikko! A Bilingual Counting*

Book (Garza, 2015), is about a topic the children could all relate to: bedtime! Nikko's mother sends him to bed, but he cannot go to sleep because there are *luchadores* battling on his bed. This is a great counting book; it is colorful and draws children in.

Rudas: Niño's Horrendous Hermanitas (Morales, 2018), the sequel to *Niño Wrestles the World,* took us back to a familiar place but with a twist. In *lucha libre* there are good guys, *técnicos*, and bad guys, *rudos*. Niño's sisters are bad guys and he needs his friends to help him win the battle against the *hermanitas*.

The final book was *Lucia the luchadora* (Garza, 2015). This is the only picture book I have been able to find about *luchadoras* (female *luchadores*). There are issues on the school playground when a group of boys tell Lucia that "girls can't be superheroes." Lucia seeks advice from her abuelita who shares a long-held secret: abuelita is a *luchadora*. It turns out that Lucia comes from a long line of *luchadoras*—the daring and brave women of Mexican *lucha libre* tradition! We had lively discussions about this book; many of the boys agreed that girls "really cannot be superheroes" while the girls countered that girls could indeed be superheroes and as a matter of fact, they were—look at Wonder Woman!

The Lucha Libre text set was fueled by the children's love of Niño. For a month, the children were deeply engaged in the books and shared stories of their family experiences involving *lucha libre* or WWE in the United States. Through our text set, we learned *lucha libre* began in Mexico, in some cases it is a family business (*The Man in the Silver Mask*), *luchadores* wear masks to keep their identity a secret, they do not fight to hurt each other, and yes, indeed, there are girl *luchadoras* and they are strong (*Rudas, Niños horrendous hermanitas,* and *Lucia the luchadora*).

More Books About Luchadores

Lucía the Luchadora and the Million Masks (2018) by Cynthia Lenore Garza. Gemma, Lucía's little sister, wants to be a *luchadora* like her big sister. When Gemma makes a hole in Lucía's special silver mask, Lucía loses her patience! Abuela decides to take them both to the *mercado* to find a *lucha libre* mask just for Gemma.

Training Day (El Toro and Friends) (2021) by Raúl the Third. We met El Toro in *¡Vamos! Let's Go to the Market,* also by Raúl the Third. In this comic-book-style story, Kooky Dooky helps *luchador* El Toro train for his next wrestling match.

Tag Team (El Toro and Friends) (2021) by Raúl the Third. *Luchadores* La Oink Oink and El Toro are the perfect tag team as they clean up together in this playful and visually stunning early reader.

Text Set: Important Latinx Women

Children need to learn about the various roles that Latinx women play in society. They need to see Latinx women in positions of power, as leaders, as people who possess strength—strength of character, mind, and ambition—and as people who can make positive change in the world.

Latinitas: Celebrating 40 Big Dreamers (2021) by Julieta Menéndez. In 40 short biographies of Latinx women from all over the U.S. and Latin America, the book explores the first small steps that set the *Latinitas* [young Latinas] off on their journeys.

Be Bold! Be Brave! 11 American Latinas who made U.S. History/¡Sé audaz, sé valiente!: 11 latinas que hicieron historia en los Estados Unidos (2020) by Naibe Reynoso. A bilingual book highlighting 11 Latinas who made U.S. history by being the first to accomplish something in the fields of politics, arts, science, sports, or medicine.

Dolores Huerta: A Hero to Migrant Workers (2012). Susan Warren tells the story of Dolores Huerta and the battle she fought to ensure fair and safe working conditions for migrant workers.

The Astronaut With a Song for the Stars: The Story of Dr. Ellen Ochoa (2019) by Julia Finley Mosca. In 1993, Ochoa became the first Hispanic woman to go to space when she served on a nine-day mission aboard the Space Shuttle Discovery.

Danza!: Amalia Hernández and El Ballet Folklórico de México (2017) by Duncan Tonatiuh. The story of Amalia Hernández, dancer and founder of El Ballet Folklórico de México.

My Name Is/Me llamo Gabriela: The life of/la vida de Gabriela Mistral (2005) by Monica Brown. The story of Gabriela Mistral, who became the first Nobel Prize–winning Latina woman.

Frida Kahlo and Her Animalitos (2017) by Monica Brown. Brown provides a look into all the *animalitos* that were a part of Frida Kahlo's life.

Viva Frida (2014) by Yuyi Morales. Morales tells Frida Kahlo's story through stunning artwork. This is a must for an illustrator study!

Books by and About Sonia Sotomayor

Sonia Sotomayor: A Judge Grows Up in the Bronx/ La juez que creció en el Bronx (2009) by Jonah Winter.

Turning Pages (2018) by Sonia Sotomayor. Sotomayor shares her life story with young readers.

Just Ask: Be Different, Be Brave, Be You (2019) by Sonia Sotomayor. Sotomayor encourages children to be themselves.

Text Set: Abuelos/Grandparents

Grandparents play a special role in the life of many children. The books in this text set are about abuelos and the relationship with their grandchildren.

Dear Abuelo (2019) by Grecia Huesca Domínguez. Juana writes letters to her abuelo who lives in Mexico and tells him all about her life in New York, including the fact that her teacher mispronounces her first name and that she is still searching for a friend.

Where Are You From? (2019) by Yamile Saied Méndez and illustrator Jaime Kim. Some kids ask, where are you *really* from? Abuelo provides a beautiful response letting the child know she is from Abuelo's love and the "love of all before us."

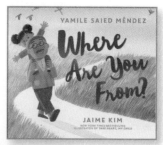

Eric Velasquez has written several books about his abuela, in Spanish and English.

Grandma's Records (2004)***/Los discos de mi abuela*** (2006). Eric spends the summer with his abuela in Spanish Harlem and learns about her favorite music—salsa. They attend a concert with Abuela's favorite band.

Grandma's Gift (2010)***/El regalo de mi abuela*** (2013). Abuela takes Eric to the Metropolitan Museum of Art where he sees a painting by Diego Velásquez and realizes for the first time that he could be an artist when he grows up. Abuela gives Eric a special Christmas gift.

Octopus Stew (2021)***/Pulpo guisado*** (2020). Abuela is cooking *pulpo guisado*, a typical Puerto Rican food, but something has gone wrong! Eric has to rescue Abuela.

Mango, Abuela, and Me (2017) by Meg Medina. Mia's abuela moves in with Mia and her parents in the city. Mia is excited to share her favorite book with Abuela and discovers that Abuela cannot read English. Mia makes a plan to teach Abuela English while Mia also learns Spanish.

Song of Frutas/Un pregón de frutas (2021) by Margarita Engle. A little girl loves visiting her grandfather in Cuba and singing his special songs to sell all kinds of fruit: *mango, limón, naranja,* and *piña.*

Playing Lotería/El juego de la lotería (2006) by Rene Colato Lainez. A little boy and his abuela discover a world of language through the game *Lotería.*

Abuelita Full of Life/Abuelita llena de vida (2007) by Amy Costales and illustrator Martha Aviles. José's Abuelita from Mexico moves in and José does not know what to expect. He discovers that abuelita is full of life and surprises.

Text Set: Nursery Rhymes

Nursery rhymes are not only fun to share, but they also teach children how language works, and help develop inferencing skills and phonological awareness.

Arroz con leche: canciones y ritmos populares de América Latina/Popular Songs and Rhymes From Latin America (1992) by Lulu Delacre.

The Cazuela That the Farm Maiden Stirred (2013) by Samantha R. Vamos. A takeoff of "the house that Jack built," this book includes a glossary of Spanish words and a recipe for *arroz con leche!*

The Piñata That the Farm Maiden Hung (2019) by Samantha R. Vamos.

The Pot that Juan Built (2011) by Nancy Andrews-Goebe.

La Madre Goose: Nursery Rhymes for los Niños (2016) by Susan Middleton Elya.

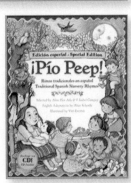

Tortillitas para Mamá and Other Nursery Rhymes (1988) by Margot Griego, Betsy Bucks, Sharon Gilbert, and Laurel Kimball.

¡Pío Peep! Traditional Spanish Nursery Rhymes Book and CD (2006) by Alma Flor Ada, F. Isabel Campoy, and Alice Schertle.

Diez Deditos and Other Play Rhymes and Action Songs from Latin America (2002) by José-Luis Orozco.

Rin, Rin, Rin/Do, re, mi: Libro ilustrado en español e inglés (2005) by José Luis Orozco.

¡Vámonos! Let's Go! (2016) by Rene Colato Laínez. Lyrical story sung to the tune of "The Wheels on the Bus."

Sing with Me/Canta conmigo: Six Classic Songs in English and Spanish (2020) by José-Luis Orozco.

Text Set: Kids Can Make a Difference

There are many things children can do to make a difference in the world. This text set lets children see that they can make a positive impact in the world.

Zonia's Rain Forest/La selva de Zonia (2021) by Juana Martínez-Neal. Zonia lives in the Amazon rain forest. One morning, the rain forest calls to her in a distressed voice. What will Zonia do? Back matter includes a translation of the story in Asháninka, information on the Asháninka community, and resources on the Amazon rain forest.

A Garden to Save the Birds (2021) by Wendy McClure. A bird flies into the glass and brother and sister Callum and Emmy learn that from the outside, the glass looks just like the sky. They also learn that the U.S. has lost a lot of birds in recent years and there are things they can do to help.

Xochitl and the Flowers/Xóchitl, la niña de las flores (2008) by Jorge Argueta and illustrator Carl Angel. Xóchitl misses the flower shop and garden her family left behind en El Salvador, so she helps them start a nursery and sell flowers on the street.

Alejandria Fights Back!/¡La lucha de Alejandria! (August 2021) by Leticia Hernandez-Linares. Nine-year-old Alejandria decides to take action and brings her community together to fight and save the neighborhood.

Maybe Something Beautiful: How Art Transformed a Neighborhood (2016) by F. Isabel Campoy and Theresa Howell. Based on the true story of the Urban Art Trail in San Diego, California, this book reveals how art can inspire transformation—and how even the smallest artists can accomplish something big.

Drum Dream Girl: How One Girl's Courage Changed Music (2015) by Margarita Engle. Inspired by the childhood of Millo Castro Zaldarriaga, a Chinese-African-Cuban girl who broke Cuba's traditional taboo against female drummers.

Sofia Valdez, Future Prez (2019) by Andrea Beaty. Sofia's abuelo walks her to school every day until one day he hurts his ankle at a local landfill and he can no longer do so. Sofia misses him and wonders what she can do about "Mount Trashmore." She gets an idea to convert the landfill into a park, but things are not that easy.

Hey, Wall: A Story of Art and Community (2018) by Susan Verde. A boy takes on a community art project in order to make his neighborhood more beautiful.

Stella Díaz Never Gives Up (Stella Diaz, Book 2) (2021) by Angela Dominguez. Stella wants to save the ocean and needs to figure out how she is going to make a difference.

Galápagos Girls/Galapagueña (2018) by Marsha Diane Arnold and illustrator Angela Dominguez. Valentina spends her days on the island where she was born observing the natural world around her. She understands the vulnerability of this wondrous world and makes a solemn promise to protect the islands and her animal friends.

Text Set: Poetry

Poetry builds community, nurtures emotional resilience, promotes literacy, and is fun! *The Poetry Friday Anthology for Celebrations: Holiday Poems for the Whole Year in English and Spanish* (2015) by Sylvia Vardell and Janet Wong is full of poems written side by side in English and Spanish about various holidays and celebrations (e.g., national pizza week, national yo-yo day), and each poem comes with a mini-lesson. The authors point out poetry's distinct benefits:

- It is accessible to a wide variety of reading abilities.
- It makes a topic more memorable through the use of vivid imagery.
- It provides a way to learn information through evocative language and rich vocabulary.
- It offers children an emotional connection and outlet for expressing themselves.
- It merges language and literacy instruction in a short burst.

Yes! We Are Latinos: Poems and Prose About the Latino Experience (2013) by Alma Flor Ada, F. Isabel Campoy, and illustrator David Diaz. Thirteen young Latinx living in the U.S. are introduced in this book celebrating the rich diversity of the Latino and Latina experience in the United States.

Imagine (2018) by Juan Felipe Herrera and illustrator Lauren Castillo. When Juan Felipe was little, he imagined what he would be when he grew up. He traveled with his family as they searched for work, learned English, and ultimately became the United States Poet Laureate!

Guacamole: Un poema para cocinar/A Cooking Poem (2016) by Jorge Argueta and illustrator Margarita Sada. A little girl sings and dances in the kitchen as she makes guacamole (recipe included).

Salsa (2017) by Jorge Argueta and illustrator Duncan Tonatiuh. A brother and sister make salsa using a *molcajete*, just like their ancestors used to do. This poem includes a recipe for salsa.

Angels Ride Bikes and Other Fall Poems/Los ángeles andan en bicicleta: Y otros poemas de otoño (2005) by Francisco Alarcón and illustrator Maya Christina González. Alarcón's poems in Spanish and English evoke childhood memories of fall in Los Angeles.

A Movie in My Pillow/Una película en mi almohada (2007) by Jorge Argueta and illustrator Elizabeth Gomez. Jorgito and his family live in San Francisco's Mission District, but he has not forgotten his native El Salvador. He has a movie in his pillow from the blending together of his new adventures and memories.

Talking with Mother Earth: Poems/Hablando con Madre Tierra: Poemas (2006) by Jorge Argueta and illustrator Lucia Angela Pérez. Tetl is different from the other children; he has brown skin, black eyes, and long hair. Tetl's journey from self-doubt to proud acceptance of his Nahuatl heritage is told in a series of poems, expressed in both English and Spanish.

Yum! ¡MmMm! ¡Qué rico! (2007) by Pat Mora and illustrator Rafael López. We are introduced to a variety of food from the Americas through Mora's haikus and López's vibrant illustrations.

Bookjoy, Wordjoy (2018) by Pat Mora and illustrator Raúl Colón. Mora has brought together a collection of her poems celebrating engaging with words and books that are accompanied by vivid illustrations that bring the poems to life.

Spicy, Hot, Colors/Colores picantes (2007) by Sherry Shahan and illustrator Paula Barrágan. With bright colors and words, this rhythmic book introduces colors in Spanish and English.

Text Set: The Fight for Justice and Equity

Children's literature is a great tool for introducing students to issues of diversity, justice, and equity. Teaching and discussing these concepts can be engaging for children. They need to know that these issues are still present today and not a thing of the past.

Soldier for Equality: José de la Luz Sáenz and the Great War (2019) by Duncan Tonatiuh. This book is about Mexican American educator, veteran, and activist José de la Luz Sáenz, the cofounder of the League of United Latin American Citizens (LULAC), a social justice organization founded in 1929 that fights for Latinx rights.

¡Sí, se puede!/Yes, We Can! Janitors Strike in L.A. (2005) by Diana Cohn and illustrator Francisco Delgado. Carlitos wonders what he can do to support his mother and the other workers who go on strike for higher wages. He decides to enlist the help of his classmates as they make signs to show their support and pride.

All Equal: A Ballad of Lemon Grove/Todos iguales: Un corrido de Lemon Grove (2019) by Christy Hale. This bilingual book tells the story of the first successful desegregation case in the United States, which took place 23 years before Brown v. Board of Education in Lemon Grove, California. The "Lemon Grove Incident" was a major victory in the battle against school segregation, and a testament to the tenaciousness of an immigrant community and its fight for equal rights.

Separate Is Never Equal: Sylvia Mendez and Her Family's Fight for Desegregation (2014) by Duncan Tonatiuh. Seven years before Brown v. Board of Education, the Mendez family fought to end segregation in California schools.

Undocumented: A Worker's Fight (2018) by Duncan Tonatiuh. Juan crosses the border into the United States and becomes an undocumented worker trying hard to survive. He gets a job busing tables at a restaurant and is severely undercompensated. Juan risks everything and stands up for himself and the rest of the community.

Side by Side/Lado a lado: The Story of Dolores Huerta and César Chávez/La historia de Dolores Huerta y César Chávez (2010) by Monica Brown and illustrator Joe Cepeda. Dolores Huerta and César Chávez motivated migrant farmworkers to fight for their rights.

Martí's Song for Freedom/Martí y sus versos por la libertad (2017) by Emma Otheguy, Adriana Domínguez, and Beatriz Vidal. A bilingual biography of José Martí, who dedicated his life to the promotion of liberty, the abolishment of slavery, political independence for Cuba, and intellectual freedom.

Text Set: Names and Identity

All names have meaning behind them. This text set engages children in thinking about their name story.

Alma and How She Got Her Name/Alma y cómo obtuvo su nombre (2018) by Juana Martínez-Neal. Martinez-Neal shares the importance of one's name and the connection to our ancestors. As she hears the story of her name, Alma starts to think it might be a perfect fit after all—and realizes that *she* will one day have her own story to tell.

René Has Two Last Names/René tiene dos apellidos (2009) by René Colato Laínez and illustrator Fabiola Graullera Ramírez. René is from El Salvador and does not understand why his name has to be different in the United States.

I Am René, the Boy/Soy René, el niño (2005) by René Colato Laínez and illustrator Fabiolla Graullera. When René's teacher calls role one morning, he is surprised to hear someone else respond to his name. It's another René, and she is a girl!

My Name Is María Isabel (1995) by Alma Flor Ada and illustrator K. Dyble Thompson. María Isabel Salazar López is new in school, and the toughest thing about being the new kid is that her teacher has decided to call her "Mary Lopez" because there are already two María's in class. Can she find a way to make her teacher see that if she loses her name, she's lost the most important part of herself?

Text Set: Immigration

I often use this timely text set on immigration. My goal in using it is to provide children with accurate information about immigration and depictions of immigrants because the media does not always do that. I also want children to learn about the positive contributions immigrants make to our country.

PICTURE BOOKS

My Shoes and I: Crossing Three Borders/Mis zápatos y yo: Cruzando tres fronteras (2019) by René Colato Laínez and illustrator Fabricio Vanden Broeck. Lainez shares his immigration story of traveling from El Salvador to the United States.

Between Us and Abuela: A Family Story From the Border (2019) by Mitali Perkins and illustrator Sara Palacios. The children have not seen their abuela in over one year. They have a special gift for her when they see her at the border fence.

Dear Abuelo (2019) by Grecia Huesca Domínguez and illustrator Teresa Martínez. A young girl writes a letter to her abuelo telling him about her adventures in her new home in the United States.

La frontera: El viaje con papá/My Journey With Papa (2018) by Deborah Mills, Alfredo Alva, and illustrator Claudia Navarro. A young boy makes the journey from Mexico to the United States with his papá.

Two White Rabbits (2015) by Jairo Buitrago and illustrator Rafael Yockteng. The story is told through the eyes of a young migrant girl making the journey north to the U.S. with her father.

Pancho Rabbit and the Coyote: A Migrant's Tale (2013) by Duncan Tonatiuh. A figurative picture book about the hardships and struggles of immigration.

Dreamers (2018) by Yuyi Morales. A beautifully illustrated memoir, this book looks at the variety of gifts that immigrants bring with them when they leave their homes. Simultaneously released in Spanish as *Soñadores*.

Mango Moon: When Deportation Divides a Family (2019) by Diane de Anda and illustrator Sue Cornelison. Told from the child's perspective, we learn about the heartbreak that families go through when a parent is deported.

Tomás and the Library Lady (1997) by Pat Mora and illustrator Raúl Colón. Tomás is the son of migrant workers who travel every summer from Texas to Iowa to follow the crops.

Friends From the Other Side/Amigos del otro lado (1997) by Gloria Anzaldúa and illustrator Consuelo Mendez. Prietita befriends Joaquin, a young boy who recently crossed the Rio Grande River to Texas in search of a new life.

El camino de Amelia (1995) by Linda Jacobs Altman and illustrator Enrique O. Sánchez. The daughter of migrant farm workers, Amelia is tired of moving and dreams of a permanent home.

Super Cilantro Girl/La Superniña del Cilantro (2003) by Juan Felipe Herrera and illustrator Honorio Robleda Tapia. Esmeralda Sinfronteras, otherwise known as Super Cilantro Girl, is a superhero who is going to rescue her mother from a migrant detention center.

Radio Man: A Story in English and Spanish (1997) by Arthur Dorros. Diego and his family are migrant farmers who follow the crops from state to state. Diego always has his radio with him, which helps him keep in touch with friends he meets on his travels.

MIDDLE GRADE BOOKS

- *They Call Me Güero: A Border Kid's Poems* (2018) by David Bowles
- *The Distance Between Us: Young Readers Edition* (2016) by Reyna Grande
- *The Only Road* (2017) by Alexandra Díaz
- *Migrant: The Journey of a Mexican Worker* (2014) by José Manuel Mateo
- *The Circuit: Stories From the Life of a Migrant Child* (1994) by Francisco Jiménez

DOCUMENTARIES (ALL THREE OF THESE ARE AVAILABLE ON YOUTUBE)

- *Through the Eyes of a Child Immigrant* (a TEDx Talk by Erik Gomez)
- *To Be Happy: An Immigrant Student's Tale* (a report on Kansas City PBS)
- *Helping Immigrant Students Adjust to New Schools, New Lives* (a video from *Education Week*)

Give Book Talks

How do we get children interested in books? How do we expose them to books they may not necessarily choose to read on their own? Book talks! For all intents and purposes, a book talk is a sales pitch. You "sell" a book or book series, hoping your students will consume it. Why do book talks? As teachers we have so many books that we love, and we simply cannot read them all to our students. Book talks are a way to whet students' appetites by providing enough information to pique their curiosity without giving away too much. You want to say just enough to get them wondering what is going on in those pages.

Book talks can be theme related (e.g., *lucha libre*, family, immigration) or content-area related (social studies, science, etc.), or they can simply be focused on books you like and that you would like students to read. (You might be noticing that your students are focusing too much of their reading time on familiar books, and you want them to try something new.) You will likely lead book talks to start, but over time you can turn them over to students and let them entice one another to read. It is important to model a book talk before letting students lead them.

Begin book talks by gathering students in a central location where they can all see the book. Hold up the book and point out something that makes it special—for example, the illustrations or the author's note. Perhaps you have read other books by the author. Talk about the genre (e.g., mystery, folktale) and connect the book talk to similar books you have read or the students liked. The goal is to "sell" them the book. Read an excerpt from the book and give students a summary, one that does not give too much away, but gets the students interested. While reading, make sure that your voice communicates excitement so they will want to explore the book further. Ask if anyone else has read the book and has commentary to offer, reminding them not to give any important plot points away. Finally, pass the book around so that students can flip through it.

Book talks are a way to whet students' appetites by providing enough information to pique their curiosity without giving away too much. You want to say just enough to get them wondering what is going on in those pages.

Book talks can also be given by guests, not always the teacher! Book talks are a great way to get families involved. If you are reading books about a topic that families are familiar with or have a background in, invite a family member to do a book talk. Going back to my experience with the *lucha libre* text set, perhaps you can find a *luchador* to give a short presentation to the class, or, at the very least, you may have a family member who knows about wrestling and is willing to come in and talk with the students. Although they may not be familiar with the book, sharing stories or what they know about the topic might be enough to interest your students. If they have been to a match, they might have photographs to share. Guest book talkers (Harvey & Ward, 2017) can also be community members, custodians, bus drivers, or cafeteria workers—how wonderful to include the school community in book talks! Book talks can also be given in any language—they are not limited to English. Imagine the joy in a child's face when their family member comes to school and speaks in Spanish. What a proud moment!

Use Latinx Literature Across the Curriculum

Students can build literacy skills while building knowledge in content areas such as science, math, and social studies. Each content area has language all its own and tools that provide information in a variety of ways (e.g., tables, graphs, maps). As children progress through school, the emphasis shifts from learning to read to reading to learn, and each content area demands strong reading and writing skills due to the nature of its language. Children's literature, including Latinx children's literature, can help you build those skills. There are several reasons for including picture books in the curriculum. I address a few of them below.

Latinx literature provides an entry point to understanding technical concepts. While textbooks are written to inform, many children's books are, too. But children's books use language in a variety of styles and forms, which is typically more engaging than a dry text book.

Latinx literature is beautiful. Illustrations support the written text and extend the meaning of the text. Picture books provide learners access both in pictures and words; the illustrations draw learners at all levels into the book.

Latinx literature is available in a variety of formats. Picture books are multimodal; they contain "dynamically interactive elements, as readers (not authors) choose where to look and how to engage with certain aspects of the text" (Hassett & Curwood, 2009). For example, *Migrant* (Mateo, 2014) tells the story of one family's journey to the United States, in a book formatted like an accordion. Readers can open the book panel by panel and follow the text or the intricate illustrations.

Latinx literature tells stories that textbooks cannot. Because they are written about one topic with illustrations providing support and extending the meaning of the words, they make complex curricular topics comprehensible and interesting. *Parrots Over Puerto Rico* (Roth & Trumbore, 2013) tells the

story of how the intrusion of human activity brought Puerto Rico's iguaca parrots to the verge of extinction. Students can learn about environmental factors, biodiversity, and the history of Puerto Rico as they engage with this book.

Latinx literature supplements textbooks. Textbooks can only provide so much information. Some topics receive only a section, a chapter, or just a paragraph, and sometimes teachers and students want more. With the variety of picture books available, it would be difficult not to find a few books on any given topic.

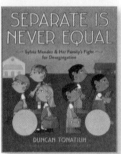

Latinx literature introduces students to voices too often missing from the curriculum. One example is *Separate Is Never Equal: Sylvia Mendez and Her Family's Fight for Desegregation* (Tonatiuh, 2014), which captures the little-known story of the Mendez family's fight for the desegregation of schools in California in 1947, and laid the groundwork for Brown v. Board of Education, the landmark decision ending segregation in the United States.

Conduct Pláticas Literarias

Pláticas literarias are literature circles (Short, 1997) where small groups of children gather to discuss books that they have read or have had read aloud to them. The *pláticas* engage children in authentic discussions about topics of interest to them and support Kathy Short's notion that "children are born language-users, naturally and eagerly talking about the things they do and are interested in." The *pláticas* provided my students a space to engage in "explicit discussions about their experiences" (Bartolomé, 2003) where they were able to think deeply about the sociopolitical realities of their lives (e.g., racism, poverty, and immigration) and tried to make sense of these issues by sharing their *cuentos*. These *pláticas* gave the children the chance to share their life *cuentos*, which connected them to each other and to the world outside of our classroom.

Why Call Them *Pláticas Literarias*?

Before going any further, I should explain the name *pláticas literarias* (López-Robertson, 2004). I was very excited about starting the discussions and gathered the children on the carpet to explain that we would be talking about books in an engagement called literature discussions. Jasmine raised her hand and said, *"¿Miss, si va ser en español, porque no lo llamamos pláticas literarias?"/*"Miss, if we are doing this in Spanish, why don't we call them *pláticas literarias*?" And that is how the children named *our* literature discussions *pláticas literarias*.

Talking With the Families

At the beginning of the school year, I invited my families to come to our classroom and browse all the books that I planned to use in our *pláticas literarias*. I had all the books available in Spanish and English. I gave a book talk on each book, explained the process we would follow in the *pláticas* and talked with the families and answered their questions. I left the books on the tables so that my families could browse them at their convenience. I also sent home monthly updates so that the families would know the topic of the month's *pláticas,* and I invited the families to come in during the *pláticas*. Because we would be discussing critical social issues, I gave my families the opportunity to opt out of any *plática* in which they did not want their child to participate; I had talked with our school librarian and she agreed to work with any child during this time. In my 14 years of engaging children in these *pláticas*, I had only one child whose family opted out of a discussion; this was during a discussion of the Day of the Dead.

It all begins with the whole-class read-aloud.

There are many ways to organize the *pláticas* and that organization depends on the teacher and students. One of the best ways that I have found for children to share their life stories is to begin with a read-aloud. Reading aloud was a very important part of my curriculum and usually took place three times a day: to open the school day, after lunch, and to close the school day. Reading aloud plays a crucial role in reading development and comprehension; it models intonation, pacing, and, for emergent bilinguals especially, it gives them the opportunity to listen to the way in which words are pronounced—it helps them hear how the language sounds. For the *pláticas literarias*, I read aloud the book to the children one day in Spanish and the following day in English—this way I was assured that the children understood the book because they were hearing it in their dominant language. The whole-class read-alouds also included discussion where the children asked questions and shared their wonderings and where they also made the connections to and between books—connections that are so necessary for children's learning.

A Rocky Start

All the *pláticas literarias* began and ended at the carpet; here we gathered to listen to the story, engaged in a discussion with one another, and shared our responses. After our first couple of *pláticas*, I was left wondering how I would ever get the children beyond "I like this part because the dog is cute" or "I like this part because I have a dress like that one." The children's behavior during these first few *pláticas* was to be expected because they had never been asked to think about books in this manner. Up until this point in school, they had not been asked to think deeply about what they were listening to or reading; they had been asked to dissect a story; tell the beginning, middle, and end and to describe the characters, the plot, the conflict, and the resolution. Because I was asking them to participate in a reading engagement that they were unfamiliar with, we struggled through the first few *pláticas*. However, because I believed that the children indeed had connections to make to these books that went beyond the "I like" statements, I did not give up!

I explained to the children that during our guided reading time, my concern was about how they read and how they were learning to become strategic readers. I then explained that during our *pláticas*, I wanted them to become critical thinkers. I wanted them to critically engage with their readings; I wanted them to think about the author's message, how they were interpreting the story, and what connections they were making to the story. I asked them to think about the following:

- Does this story remind you of anything or anyone that you know?
- Has something similar happened in your life?
- What connections are you making to your life and the life of your family?
- What connections are you making to other things we have read or talked about?
- What are your questions and wonderings?

I was guiding them to think about what was in their hearts. For each discussion, I taped a piece of butcher paper on the board and wrote the children's wonderings, questions, and connections; this served to guide our discussions and was also a way to demonstrate to all of my children that their voices and opinions mattered. When we first began the *pláticas*, I would stop periodically while reading and ask the children if they had connections or anything that they wanted to share with the class. As they became more used to the discussions, the children would simply share and ask questions while I read. I paused between pages to give them time to think and respond aloud if they chose. We also did a lot of "turn and talk" where they would turn to the person next to them and share one thing they were thinking about. I learned early on that although I wanted to hear what they were thinking, I had to provide a structure; otherwise, we would spend the day in the read-aloud!

On the second day of discussion, I read the book in English and we continued in the same format. The discussion on the second day was always richer than the first day; since the butcher paper from yesterday's discussion was still up on the board, it provided the children a reference point. Because they had time to think about and process the story, the second day's discussion usually produced more wonderings. After the whole-class discussion, I asked the children to go to their tables for the individual responses.

Individual Responses

I gave each child a piece of manila construction paper, 5 x 7 inches, and asked him or her to think about the questions that guided our discussions (the questions on page 106):

- Does this story remind you of anything or anyone that you know?
- Has something similar happened in your life?
- What connections are you making to your life and the life of your family?
- What connections are you making to other things we have read or talked about?
- What are your questions and wonderings?

On one side of the paper, they wrote their responses and on the other they drew their responses (see the examples on the following pages). I think that educators sometimes forget the power of drawing and try to steer children

away from drawing. Drawing, however, is a form of writing (Ray & Cleveland, 2004) and it is an especially important form of communication for emergent bilinguals and for young children.

While discussing *Tomás and the Library Lady/Tomás y la señora de la biblioteca* (Mora, 1997), the children were struck by the fact that Tomás and his brother went to the dump to look for books and toys. They wanted to do something to help our community and decided to hold a canned food and gently used toy drive in our school. On the last day of school before holiday break, we loaded up about 10 wagons and together with a few parents walked to the food pantry near our school. We were met by the director who had my students categorize the canned food items and toys and fill the pantry. Upon returning to school, we talked a lot about the connections to *Tomás and the Library Lady*. I asked the children to write about our experience.

RESPONSE 1 TRANSLATED FROM SPANISH:

I felt sad because I was looking at the people without food and clothes because they are poor and I was happy because we helped the poor children and the men and women and I am very sad because some children want something for Christmas and you don't have it, poor children what I want most is that there are no more poor

> Yo me senti triste Porque estava biendo a la Jente
> Sin Comiday Sin ropa Porque Son Pobres Y Yo
> me senti Fele Porque les ayudamos a los niños
> Pobres Y a los Señorez y Señoras y estoy muy triste
> Porque algunos niños Quieren algo para navidad Y
> no lo tienes Pobres niños lo Que yo mas
> Quirio Que no aiga nadich Pobres en
> el mundo ¿Porqué? ay gente Pobre en el
> mundo eso es lo que yo mismo me Pregoto.
> Porque ay Jente Pobre en el mundo
> Viridiana 11-28-000

Response to *Tomás and the Library Lady/Tomás y la señora de la biblioteca*

people in the world. Why are there poor people in the world? That is what I ask myself, why are there poor people in the world?

RESPONSE 2 TRANSCRIBED FROM ENGLISH:

I felt like a hero to help the poor. I felt kind of embarrassed too! But I thought that was nice and I felt sad when I saw all the people waiting for food. I am happy!

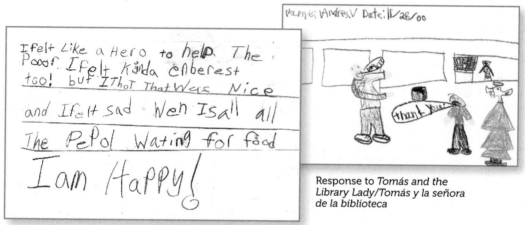

Response to *Tomás and the Library Lady/Tomás y la señora de la biblioteca*

Small-Group **Pláticas Literarias**

While the class was working, I'd pull a small group of students for the *plática literaria*. During these groups, the children had the chance to share their thoughts, wonderings, and questions in a much smaller setting. As much as possible, I participated in the groups rather than lead them; however, for the first few *pláticas*, I took on the teacher role. I made sure everyone had a chance to speak, that students listened to one another, and that they took turns speaking. I had noticed that the children were so eager to share their thoughts that once someone finished a sentence, the next child jumped in to share their thoughts. I modeled careful listening. I asked the children to look at the person who was speaking and, rather than talking immediately after they were finished, to take a few moments to sit with what was said. After a few moments, I asked them to respond to what was just said. The children were not being dismissive of the speaker; they simply did not know how to listen carefully and purposefully. Once they stopped to listen, they were able to connect with the book and with one another. It was in these groups that I learned about the power of story and how my young students used storytelling to make sense of their lives (López-Robertson, 2004).

I rotated small groups over the next several days until each of my students participated in a small-group discussion. At the end of the day's discussions, as a mini-wrap-up, I invited a few children who had completed their written and illustrated responses to share their responses with the class. While they shared, I wrote further wonderings that sprung from the sharing on the butcher paper that by this time had become two or three pieces of butcher paper.

Whole-Group Sharing

Once our small-group discussions were over, the class gathered on the carpet again for a final discussion of the focus book. By this time most of the children had shared their written and illustrated responses with the class. For those remaining, they came to the front of the room and shared their art and thinking with the class. The others listened and asked questions and made connections with one another's responses. We wrapped up each discussion with a summary of the book and a review of the original butcher paper containing their wonderings, questions, and connections (WQC). The children noted if we had provided responses to all the WQC's. If we missed

any, now was the time to provide a response. If there was something that we could not answer at this time, we moved it to another piece of butcher paper that was labeled *"preguntas para otro tiempo"*/ "questions for another time." Because the discussions were about the socio-political realities of their lives, and the children and their families were deeply invested, we took a week or so off from the discussions and engaged in other curricular activities related to the unit of study.

Morning meeting in my second-grade classroom

A Classroom Example of a *Plática Literaria* About Migrant Farmworkers

We were studying migrant farmworkers in my second-grade class because of the children's interest in where fruits and vegetables came from. Originally, we engaged in a plant unit as did all the second grades in the school district. While reviewing the section on how vegetables grow, one of my students, David, offered that "they came from his uncle," specifically from the farm where his uncle worked. I was not following what he was saying, so he explained that his uncle "works on the farm up north and puts the seeds [in the ground], waters them and when the fruit comes out, he picks them and then they are sold." Another child, Miguel, offered that his uncle must be rich because there are so many vegetables in the store, and he must make a lot of money.

Sofía: *Sí, pero no es de él. Él trabaja para un señor y el señor le paga al tío, yo sé porque mi prima y su familia también están allá.*

Yes, but it is not his. He works for a man and he pays [David's] uncle, I know because my cousin and her family are also there.

Miguel: *¿Cómo es eso? ¿Cómo tu tío no vende la fruta y tiene dinero para su familia?*

How is that? How come your uncle doesn't sell the fruit and have money for his family?

Sofía: *Porque son trabajadores de la tierra. Ellos hacen eso para el dueño de la granja.*

Because they are farm workers. They do the work for the owner of the farm.

All my students were excitedly talking at the same time about people they knew who were *"trabajadores de la tierra"*/"farm workers." They had so much to say and had so many questions that from this exchange, our unit on migrant farm workers grew. We watched video documentaries, had several guest speakers—some family members and others prominent people in our community who came to share their experiences, conducted research, and read and talked about many books.

Five children and I were engaged in a small-group discussion about the book *El camino de Amelia* (Altman, 1993). Amelia Luisa is tired of moving from town to town with her family as they search for fields where they will work all day and Amelia will start at a new school again. She dreams of a house with a large tree in the yard that she can call home and where she will no longer need to drive on unknown roads. Jomaira shared how she had found a box one day, like Amelia had done in the book, and how she, too, had hidden special *"cositas que me encontraba"* things she had found in the box. She told us how she buried the box, but her dog, Chata, dug it up. Gabriela also connected to finding a box and hiding it like Amelia had in the story and added that after cleaning her box, *"porque tenía mucha tierra y le eché la foto que hice yo misma, eche un nombre mío, y una flor"*/"it was full of dirt and I added a picture that I made, my name, and a flower." Katie asked her, "Which flower?" Gabriela responded, *"Son unas flores, son rojas y tenía una mariposa. Sabe el libro* La mariposa*, así se miraba la mariposa, igualita"*/"They were red flowers and had a butterfly. You know the book *La mariposa*, like that, it looked just like that butterfly." In her response, Gabriela connected to another book we had read in our migrant farm workers unit—*La mariposa* (Jiménez, 2000).

Pláticas literarias provided my students the opportunity to engage in discussions about topics with which they could identify, in the language of their choice, and as a teacher, I was able to draw on their "cultural ways of knowing and making meaning" (López-Robertson, 2012). The children demonstrated that they were active thinkers seeking to make meaning from the books we read; they created written and illustrated responses, demonstrating their ability to make necessary connections between the books they read and their own life experiences, and they actively participated in discussions.

Concluding Thought

Children have the right to see accurate representations of themselves, their families, and their cultures in their school curricula. Additionally, they need to broaden their worlds by being exposed to and engaging with Latinx literature. I hope the strategies and text sets presented in this chapter provide a guide for how to begin to use that literature in your classroom.

Chapter Five

¡Bienvenidos!/Welcome In!

Engaging Families in Classrooms and Schools

Recently, when I walked into the office of a local school for a meeting with a principal, I noticed a Spanish-speaking mother trying to communicate with the English-speaking receptionist. Although she tried using all the English at her disposal, the mother was unsuccessful at expressing her needs. The receptionist, clearly frustrated, kept repeating, "I don't speak Spanish. English. Say it in English." The mother was flustered, on the verge of tears. I approached her and asked if I could be of assistance. Her face brightened and with a sigh of relief, she accepted my offer.

A reminder: Latinx literature is not just for classrooms and schools with Latinx children. It should be available to all children in all communities.

Why share this story? For children and their families to feel welcome in our schools, it must start at the front door. Even if no staff members speak a language other than English, they should be respectful and try to communicate with families to the best of their ability. Of the many things I found interesting about the exchange I witnessed was that the Latinx mother was *trying* to communicate, but the receptionist was not listening or trying to make sense of what the mother was trying to say. Instead, she repeatedly made it clear that the mother needed to speak in English and that she was not welcome, reminding me that "institutional racism is not only characterized by race; it is also based on ethnicity, language, color, gender, sexuality, poverty, and immigration status" (Bernal & Alemán, 2017).

Latinx Families and the Power of Literature

In this chapter, I provide suggestions for engaging Latinx families in schools and creating welcoming spaces, using Latinx literature, based on my experience as a classroom teacher and a university researcher. A reminder: Latinx literature is not just for classrooms and schools with Latinx children. It should be available to all children in all communities. Before I begin that discussion, I address some common misconceptions about Latinx families because they can impact the way Latinx children are viewed, treated, and taught in schools.

Common Misconceptions About Latinx Families

Misconception 1: They Do Not Value Their Children's Education Latinx immigrants come to the United States seeking a better future for themselves and their children. One way to achieve that is to pursue an education, which is not available to the general public in many Latin American countries. While some sort of free public education is available in most countries, a full-time, high-quality education is often reserved for those who can afford to pay for it. Education, then, is a commodity that is very valuable to the majority of Latinx families.

My own parents always stressed the importance of an education and, while they were unable to pursue one for themselves, they made sure my siblings and I had one. My father always said *"Estudia, es lo único que te puedo dejar que nadie te lo pueda quitar"*/"Study! School is the only thing I can leave you that no one can take away." Both of my parents came to the United States seeking a better life and, like most Latinx parents, they had high expectations for their children and their education (Delgado-Gaitán, 2004; Nieto, 2004; Ada & Zubizarreta, 2001). However, because of the mismatch between their own school experiences and those of the people born in the

Mother and daughter drawing during our illustrator study

United States, Latinx families may not demonstrate support for education in a way that is familiar to mainstream American educators.

Were it not for my family's support and belief in my academic potential, I may not have attended university at all, much less have earned a doctorate. As a high school student, I was strong academically. I took advanced courses, was a member of the National Honor Society, and was in the top five percent in my graduating class. Regardless, my guidance counselor advised me numerous times to attend beauty school because, as she said, "Hispanics do not finish school, so at least you will have a trade," clearly demonstrating that deficit "discourses and practices often persist in the professional lives of educators and permeate school buildings across the country" (Bernal & Alemán, 2017). Because my parents knew the value of an education and instilled it in my siblings and me, I did not shortchange myself by listening to my guidance counselor. My mother had a saying that carried me and continues to carry me through life: *Pa'lante, pa'lante, pa'tras ni pa' coger impulso,* which roughly translates to "Forward, forward, no going back, not even for momentum."

Misconception 2: They Resist Enrolling Their Children in Pre-Kindergarten Programs When it comes to this misconception, we need to look at systemic issues, specifically transportation and access to information. PreK is not available in all areas and if it is, most districts do not offer transportation, leaving families responsible for it. Another complicating factor is that where preK is offered, it is usually only a half-day program and, again, this leaves families to not only deal with transportation, but also conflicts with work.

Misconception 3: They Do Not Have High Expectations for Their Children While some Latinx families may not behave in a way that mainstream culture expects when it comes to school, that is by no means an indication that they do not have high expectations for their children. As noted above, the vast majority of Latinx families value education and do whatever they can to help their children be successful. Alma Flor Ada and Rosalma Zubizarreta (2001) offer that "it is a given that they [Latinx families] want their children to continue their schooling and attain a professional career." It is deficit thinking on the part of the school to believe otherwise.

Señora Herron,

Thank you for the books that you lent Dylan. We read them together every night and he is very interested in listening. I hope that you continue to send us books so that we can continue reading them. You are doing an exceptional job with my son. We see he is learning so much and we, my wife and I, are so happy. Thank you.

Misconception 4: They Resist Learning English and Assimilating Into "American" Culture Many Latinx families maintain their home language as a means of remaining connected to their home country, culture, and family. It is important to remember the importance of linguistic identity and the pride that it can bring. Anzaldúa (1997) writes, "until I can take pride in my language, I cannot take pride in myself." Because one wants to maintain Spanish does not mean that he or she does not want to learn English. Quite the contrary: Latinx families know that to be successful in the United States, one must be fluent in English, the language of power. Although they may "struggle in developing a degree of proficiency in English" (Springer, Hollist, & Buchfink, 2009), Latinx families understand the importance of their children becoming fluent in English.

Being able to communicate and make sense of the world in two languages and cultures are examples of funds of knowledge that many Latinx children possess. However, as noted in Chapter One, while some Latinx children are bilingual, we cannot presume they all are. Families typically weigh several factors when deciding on whether to maintain their native language, most related to personal experiences and struggles. For example, some families may believe their children will be at a disadvantage by speaking Spanish. Some fear their children will suffer ridicule or discrimination. Families who abandon their native language generally do it for clear reasons and feel it is in their children's best interest. All families, regardless of native language, want their children to live a safe, happy, successful, and peaceful life, including Latinx families. Whether they retain their native language, they all pass a significant part of their cultural heritage onto their children, consciously or unconsciously.

Misconception 5: They Are Unwilling to Participate in Their Children's Education This misconception may have more to do with the school community than Latinx families. In many parts of Latin America, teachers are revered and seen as the expert responsible for educating the child, and parents are responsible for overseeing the child's home life. Direct participation is not always suggested or expected. In the United States, many Latinx parents do not participate not because they are unwilling, but because they have limited experiences with schooling in the United States. Researcher Delgado Gaitán (2014) explains, "the knowledge of what and how parents need to negotiate with the school to advocate for their children is often culturally bound." However, there is ample evidence that when Latinx families develop an understanding of cultural expectations, and feel welcome in the school community, they are willing to become active stakeholders. (Delgado Bernal & Alemán, 2017; Alvarez, 2017).

Samantha's Story:
An Example of Family Participation

Many years ago, when I was teaching second grade, I engaged my students in a unit on plants, which was part of the required curriculum. I asked the students, "Where do vegetables come from?" and one of them responded,

> *Vienen de allá de donde mi tío Joaquín. Allá en la granja, él las jala de las plantas como tomates, frijoles y unas veces repollos. Y las ponen en unas cajas y luego el gerente los vende en la tienda.*

> They come from over there, from my uncle Joaquin. There on the farm. He pulls them from plants—tomatoes, beans, and sometimes cabbage. And then puts them in crates, and the owner sells them at the store.

While I thought I was prepared for the plant unit, David made me realize I was not entirely, as I mentioned in the discussion of *plática literarias* on page 111. I had not once considered the "human" side of growing plants because I was focusing mainly on the science of plants. The children shifted my focus to "*trabajadores de la tierra*" migrant farm workers. I had extremely limited knowledge of that population and, as such. I would be learning right alongside the children.

As the weeks progressed, the children read books about plants and growing plants, listened to books, and participated in *pláticas*, watched documentaries, searched for more information, and welcomed visitors who came to talk to us about their experiences working in the fields. While I had been engaging the children in investigations and inquiries since the beginning of the year, this one was different. Children who tended to be reserved and, at times, disengaged, really got into this unit. At one point, one of the children, Samantha, shared what she and her family had done over the weekend: visited a migrant camp. "*Hicimos como Juan en el libro*"/"We did like Juan in the book," she said, referring to *Calling the Doves/El canto de las palomas* by Juan Felipe Herrera (1995), the book we had read and talked about the week before.

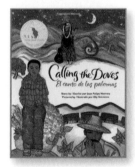

At dismissal, Señora Rivera, Samantha's mother, and I had a great talk. Samantha's mother explained that Samantha "*me tenía loca con esto de los trabajadores de la tierra*"/"was driving her crazy talking about the farmworkers and Juan and his family." Her husband had a friend who worked on a big farm and had extended an invitation to visit. After some pleading from Samantha, Señora Rivera and the family got in the car and drove about one hour north to the farm *"para que ella vea con sus propios ojos"*/"so that Samantha could see what it was with her own eyes." Earlier Samantha had told the class how her back hurt and her hands were sore because she had worked the farm. Señora Rivera explained that she felt compelled to do something to answer all Samantha's questions and felt the best thing to do was to take them to the farm. She explained that *"fue una gran lección para toda la familia"*/"it was a great lesson for the whole family." When children are interested in a unit of study and when we include "families' experiences, reflections, and wisdom" (Ada & Zubizarreta, 2001) and find ways to integrate family and family's ways of knowing, everyone benefits.

Core Beliefs About Families

Karen Mapp, Ilene Carver, and Jessica Lander (2017) discuss four core beliefs that guide work with families:

- All families have dreams and aspirations for their children.
- All families can be equal partners in their children's education.
- All families have the capacity to support their children's learning.
- Schools must take the first step in building partnerships with families.

Those core beliefs are asset-based and recognize that all families, regardless of linguistic, cultural, or socioeconomic background, have the capacity to support, encourage, and teach their children. They align well with suggestions for working with Latinx families.

All Families Have Dreams and Aspirations for Their Children

I work with a phenomenal classroom teacher, María del Rocío Herron, who was my youngest son's preK teacher more than 10 years ago. I enjoy spending time in her classroom with her four-year-old students and their families. Rocío was concerned that her Latinx families were not understanding the school's vision for and approach to reading instruction. So, with a few other teachers, she organized a bilingual family literacy night for Latinx families with children in preK to grade one. The goal of the event was to familiarize the families with the reading expectations. The teachers did that by engaging family members in literacy centers like the ones their children engaged in daily. They provided childcare for the children in another part of the building, so that families could focus on what was being shared. The event began with a warm welcome and a review of the evening's schedule: read-aloud, centers, and dinner.

I read aloud *Soñadores* (2018) by Yuyi Morales and then showed a short video interview with Morales herself discussing the book. Both the book and interview were in Spanish, which delighted the families. In the discussion following the read-aloud and interview, the families shared dreams they had for their children: "*Quiero que sea feliz y que realice sus sueños*"/"I want her to be happy and realize her dreams." "*Que vaya al colegio como yo no pude*"/"To go to college, as I could not." Latinx families have dreams and aspirations for their children, just like any family.

Families creating artifacts during a family literacy night

All Families Can Be Equal Partners in Their Children's Education

Once families know the expectations for participating in their child's education, they will meet and, in many cases, exceed those expectations. Schools must do a better job of communicating expectations to families and letting them know that they matter and that they will be heard. We must recognize that everyone, both faculty members and families, has something valuable to offer, and everyone needs to understand that he or she is working for the common good of the school.

All Families Have the Capacity to Support Their Children's Learning

Teachers need to view families as assets—as competent, capable, and active participants in their child's schooling. All families possess and bring funds of knowledge (González, Moll, and Amanti, 2006), cultural- and community-specific knowledge, and a variety of ways to make meaning. You can use those funds of knowledge to cocreate culturally relevant curriculum that connects home and school. As Concha Delgado-Gaitan (2001) notes, "Culture, when affirmed and shared, creates possibilities for building bridges."

Schools Must Take the First Step in Building Partnerships With Families

Patricia Edwards (2016) talks about families having "ghosts" of school past. In other words, for some families, particularly families of color, school may not have been a positive place to be, and therefore they may be reluctant to enter a relationship with you and your colleagues. The ghosts of their past prevent them from trusting schools. However, we must persevere and not give up on connecting with families. If you speak Spanish, terrific. If you don't, use human translators, electronic translators, or a combination of both. It takes time to build trust with families. Once they see that you are trying, and that your best interest is with their children, your persistence will pay off.

Working With Latinx Families

Beliefs are important, and so is action. In this section, I answer critical questions such as, How do we engage Latinx families in schools? How do we create welcoming spaces in our schools for Latinx families?

Ensure Families Feel They Belong to and Are Integral to the School Community

To create a strong partnership between schools and families, we must work from a foundation of mutual respect and trust, understanding that the process takes time. The goal is to create schools that are central to the larger community and places where families want to spend time because they feel safe and valued. For that to happen, we must seek to understand.

Latinx parents creating books with their children

Each family comes from a different situation, so we must treat each one individually and with respect. We need to take time to get to know families and focus on them rather than on "disparate programs that are disconnected from instructional practice and school turnaround strategies" (Weiss, Lopez, & Rosenberg, 2010). Families need to know they matter. They also need to know that their way of making meaning matters.

Given the number of responsibilities classroom teachers have, family engagement can seem like one more thing to add to a very long to-do list. But it is worth it. The more welcome and valued families feel, the more likely they are to understand and participate in their children's education, which is likely to have a positive effect on their academic performance. So, consider hosting an evening designed to support families in getting to know one another and to discuss their children.

Commit to Learning From Families Instead of "Teaching" Them

Families have many things to teach us. Often, they do not realize that they are doing things at home that support their children's literacy. Help them notice those things—and encourage them to keep doing them. Rather than telling families what they need to do to help their child, listen to them. Learn about their goals for their children's academics and help them achieve them.

Recognize That Families Have Strengths and Much to Offer

Families are a child's first teacher and provide children with the foundation upon which everything is built. As teachers, we need to recognize and value that. Invite families to share stories with your class. Ask them to read aloud to the children. Ask them to share skills they have that may be of interest to the children, such as sewing, gardening, and cooking. When I was teaching, I remember Hector's mother, who was a fantastic cook, came in to make *albóndiga* soup/meatball soup. I wrote out the recipe on chart paper, and the children followed along, helping with measuring, chopping, and stirring. For all intents and purposes, it was a math, literacy, and science lesson all rolled into one and led by a child's mother. Seeing the pride on Hector's face as his mother taught the class was priceless!

Home Visits

Home visits help create a positive relationship between the family, student, and teacher and can open the doors for communication and collaboration. Meeting in classrooms can be intimidating for some families and in traveling to the family home, the power dynamic shifts from the family being on "our turf" [the school] to a comfortable and safe place, their home. Families feel more at ease being in their home and are more likely to speak more openly. While in the home, our goal should be to interact and engage with the family and get to know its members. Your role during a home visit is as a learner. You are not there to teach anything; you are there to listen and learn. An important goal of the home visit is for our students and their family members to realize that there is a network of support. We are here to help them. We go to the home seeking to understand the family and student's environment to better help her or him in school. Our focus is on building a relationship, extending support, and actively listening to the family's concerns and insights.

As a teacher, I did home visits twice a month—they were required in the school where I taught. Through the visits, I was able to name the activities the families were engaging in with their children, and it was there that I learned that Hector's mother was a fantastic cook and asked her to visit our class and cook with the children. Those visits also helped me to build a trusting relationship with families.

Engage All Families

Some families may be harder to connect with. But do not give up on them. Even if some families fail to respond, continue to send them invitations to classroom events, as well as more casual invitations to stop by when they can. For many families, it was difficult to attend events during the school day because of work. To accommodate them, I varied the times of events so that all families had a chance to attend. I did some before school, at lunch, after school, and in the evening.

Talk With Families and Listen to Their Concerns

We were a few months into a new school year, and Rocío, the teacher with whom I work, was concerned about her Latinx families. Some of the mothers were feeling left out and not a part of the school community. Rocío and I decided to invite them to a literacy night at school and when asked what they could bring, we responded they could bring a dessert to share. In return, we provided childcare, so they did not need to worry about the children. Our goal was to create community for the mothers, a safe and welcoming forum for them to voice their concerns and share their opinions and stories.

After introductions, we proceeded with a read-aloud; I read *Playing Lotería/El juego de la lotería* (2006) by René Colato Laínez. We chose the book because we knew the families had at some point played *lotería* (it is a traditional game similar to bingo but uses images on a deck of cards instead of numbers). I read aloud and paused every few pages as the mothers connected to the story. They shared stories of playing *lotería* when they were younger, of winning prizes, and of some games going on for a long time. We finished the book and the mothers continued sharing stories of other games they played when they were younger and that they were now teaching their children. They also talked about fingerplays and songs they did with their children, like *los pollitos dicen*.

A little time had passed, and the conversation was slowing down. Rocío asked the mothers if they would like to talk about any issues or questions they had about school. After a few moments of silence, one mother began talking. From there, the others joined. We listened carefully and did not interrupt them. Their main point throughout the evening was that they were ready to work with their children and needed help in understanding the expectations the school had for them. As the conversation wound down, the mothers thanked us for getting them together and listening to them. They also expressed interest in getting together more often. We closed the evening by sharing our desserts and stories. Because of my read-aloud and the discussion it inspired, Rocío and I began to build a relationship with the mothers. They felt comfortable expressing what concerned them and what excited them about the year. They felt heard.

Estamos haciendo la tarea/
We Are Doing Our Homework!

As noted earlier, when I was a student, I never saw my culture, language, or community represented anywhere in my school or in the books we read. As a teacher, I engaged my students (and their families) in weekly literature discussions (see Chapter Four). Also, because I wanted families to be active participants in our classroom, I invited them in at the beginning of each grading period to review the books we would be reading for literature discussions, usually around five, among other instructional matters. I explained my procedures for literature discussions, gave a brief book talk on each of the books, and took questions. Little did I know that a group of mothers would engage in weekly *pláticas* outside our school!

On my way to school one day, I came upon the crossing guard who happened to be my student Samantha's mother, and noticed that she was holding something familiar under her left arm. It was the book *Pepita Talks Twice/Pepita habla dos veces* (Lachtman, 1995), which I had sent home with the children a few days earlier as part of the homework with a request that an adult at home read the book with the child and help the child write a response to the book in his or her discussion log. Then I looked to my right and noticed some beach chairs, an umbrella, and four mothers of other students, each holding their own copy of *Pepita Talks Twice/Pepita habla dos veces*. I pulled alongside the group and asked what was up. All the mothers smiled, and replied, *"¡Mis, estamos haciendo la tarea!"*/"Miss, we are doing our homework!" They explained that their children had told them their assignment. Sra. León explained that since they all had the same homework, they decided to do it together and that the best time was after they dropped the children off at school! Apparently, they met four mornings a week to read and talk about the books that we were discussing in class. Sadly, this was 17 years ago, before smartphones, and I did not have a camera, so I do not have a photograph. But I remember this day like it was yesterday!

As Alma Flor Ada and Rosalma Zubizarreta (2001) assert, "By inviting parents' experiences, reflections, and wisdom, we elicit their valuable contributions and help bridge the gap between them and their children, and between them and the schools." The mothers took it upon themselves to create their own learning space, connect their lives to my curriculum, and bridge that gap.

A parent's entry in a discussion log

Translation: This book showed me that it is important to speak two or more languages and that instead of being mistreated, it should be something of great pride and we can help different people with what we know. This book left me thinking about my three children that, with God's help and attending a bilingual school, they will develop English and Spanish and that they help us now with translation and with our lives. In my life it [the book] reminded me that I never thought that my children would be born in the U.S. and that we would live here and, that sooner or later, they would be bilingual. My connection was that in the future, my children will be bilingual and great persons.

Latinx Families as Advocates

At one point in my teaching career, my principal stopped by my classroom to inform me that I would be teaching a combination first- and second-grade class, beginning the following week. She explained that enrollment was down, and she could not justify a classroom of only 12 students. Because I had the smallest class of all the second grades, I was chosen for the combination class. I had never taught a combination class before and questioned my ability to teach two different grade levels simultaneously.

At the end of the school day, as I did every day, I sat with my students outside the classroom, waiting for them to be picked up by siblings, friends, or their parents. It was a great way to get to know important people in their lives. Diana's mother, Sra. García, arrived and we struck up a conversation. She asked me about an event that was planned for the following week, which I completely forgot about because I was so consumed by the news my principal delivered earlier in the day. I shared the news with Sra. García, and she was not pleased with the combo class idea. She explained that her nephew was in a combination class at another school and that his mother felt he was not learning what he should as a third grader because the teacher was teaching to the second graders. Sra. García said she was going to speak to the other mothers. She was not going to allow the school to jeopardize the children's education because there was a problem with the number of children in the classroom.

At the end of the school day, as I did every day, I sat with my students outside the classroom, waiting for them to be picked up by siblings, friends, or their parents. It was a great way to get to know important people in their lives.

The following week, when I was to begin teaching both grades, my principal again appeared in my classroom. She did not look happy, "Mrs. López-Robertson," she said. "I just got off the phone with Mr. Sanchez from the District Office. Apparently, your students' mothers have made several calls over the past few days expressing their displeasure about their children being in a combination class." I was shocked! I could not believe what I was hearing! "We have decided that you will retain your second-grade classroom. Be advised, though, from this point forward, every new second grader who comes to the school will be your student." Wow! Sra. García meant what she said about doing something. That year I went from having 12 second graders to 22!

This is an example of Latinx families acting as advocates for their children's education. My students' families felt a strong sense of belonging and ownership. They were involved in all aspects of school. Family input was sought and listened to, and families were respected. We all shared the same goals: to provide a safe, nurturing, and challenging learning environment for the children.

Concluding Thought

We educators need to view all families through an asset-based lens. We need to recognize that all families, regardless of linguistic, cultural, or socioeconomic background, have something positive to contribute to their children's education and to the school community. We need to remember that Latinx families, particularly immigrant families, may not fully understand the role they can play in their children's education. That means we must be explicit in our expectations, while recognizing the strengths of every family. If the expectation is for Latinx families to engage in school, then we need to explain what that means and what it looks like.

Family engagement is more than asking families to contribute to the bake sale, come to parent/teacher conferences, or attend a cultural or sporting event. We need to think beyond the 4F's: food, folklore, fashion, and festivals (Banks & Banks, 1993). We need to recognize the Latinx community in our schools not just during Hispanic Heritage Month, much in the same way African American families must be recognized beyond Black History Month.

Family engagement means working together to achieve shared goals. Where do we begin? By creating spaces in which families feel welcome, respected, and heard. Invite families to school to share their stories. Listen as they express concerns, take notes, and seek solutions with them. When Latinx families feel welcome, respected, and heard in the school, their role shifts from participant to leader and advocate. When we work as partners, children are more likely to succeed academically, and the school belongs to everyone. We cannot educate children alone. We need our families.

Chapter Six

Llamada a la acción/
A Call to Action

Pedro: ¿Mami, porqué *Latinx*?

Mami, why Latinx?

Me: Se usa la *X* para ser más inclusivo con todas las personas. Es... (interrupted)

The X is used to be more inclusive. The...

Pedro: Tomás, come here. Look at Mami's computer.

Tomás: ¿Mami, porque la *X*? Ningunos de mis amigos usan la *X*. Eso no está bien. Mis amigos son mexicanos, *Puerto Ricans* o cubanos, nadie es *Latinx*.

Mami, why the X? None of my friends use an X. That is not right. My friends are Mexican, Puerto Rican, or Cuban, no one is Latinx.

Me: Es para incluir a todas las personas. Se usa... (interrupted)

It is to include all people. It is used...

Pedro: Mami, el español es *gendered*, así es el español.

Mami, Spanish is gendered, that is how Spanish is.

Tomás: Sí. Cambiarlo y usar la *X* es *U.S. imperialism*, es dejar que los blancos cambien el español, ellos no controlan el español. Yo entiendo ser inclusivo, pero nadie quien conozco, muchachos o viejitos usan la *X*. Eso no está bien. Español es así. *Imperialism*.

Yeah. Changing and using the X is U.S. imperialism. It's letting the whites change Spanish. They don't control Spanish [language]. That is not right. Spanish is like that. Imperialism.

Pedro: Mami, hay gente que usa *Latinx* y no tiene nada que ver con ser inclusivo. Sí, *imperialism*.

Mami, there are people who use Latinx and it has nothing to do with being inclusive. Yes, imperialism.

Tomás: Mira/*look*.

Tomás took out his phone and played a video of some friends playing a game and talking about Latinx. There were four players. Out of nowhere one of them said, "Hey, what do you think about Latinx?" "Latin, what?" Another replied, "It's what they are trying to call us." "I ain't no Latinx, I am Mexican." "Yeah, and I am Puerto Rican. *Latinx* is not a word, it's made up. They just want to take over our language."

This exchange is from the conversation my sons and I had when I asked them, individually, to look at some mock-ups of covers for this book. I was completely surprised by the passion and similarities of their responses regarding the term *Latinx*. Both felt it is a form of imperialism supporting DeGuzmán's (2017) assertion that Latinx is an "example of Anglophone U.S. imperialism's corruption of the Spanish language." Additionally, my son offered evidence, via the video of his friends playing games, that no one he knows uses Latinx and that most people prefer to be referred to by national origin terms (e.g., Mexican, Puerto Rican). I self-identify as Latina and I use the term *Latinx* to demonstrate a "respect for basic human dignity" (Salinas &

My sons Tomás (19) and Pedro (15) playing at the beach

Lozano, 2019) while Sonia Nieto, in the foreword, used *Latin@* and Alma Flor Ada, noted Cuban scholar, prefers *Latine* (personal communication, May 2, 2021); all are different terms that share a desire to be inclusive and respectful of all people. As I stated early in the book, the *x* in *Latinx* is a complex issue and one that continues to be debated, even in my home!

Why share the story? To demonstrate the dynamism of language and culture; it is always changing. To reiterate the power in naming, we must provide children and families the opportunity to name themselves, and as their teachers, we must find out who they are by *asking* them. And finally, we must remember that we cannot lump all people who speak Spanish or have Spanish-sounding surnames into *one* group because we run the risk of promoting a single narrative of Latinx communities. Latinx communities are varied—there is no one Latinx community.

The purpose of this chapter is to bring everything together with a focus on advocacy, which includes awareness and praxis.

Advocacy: Taking Action to Create Change

Mahatma Gandhi said, "Be the change you wish to see in the world." Studying and promoting Latinx children's literature is a professional and personal endeavor for me. I advocate for that literature's rightful place in the curriculum because I do not want any child to feel the invisibility or disconnection at school that I did. I am an advocate for all children and especially for children who have their "native language and culture demeaned, omitted, or excluded in schools" (Berzins & López, 2001). Children should not long to see themselves in the curriculum. They should be present in it, in the library, and in the school community—and represented accurately and sensitively.

Awareness

For change to take place, there must be recognition that something needs to be changed. Briefly outlining the history of the education of Latinx children in the United States in Chapter One provided the basis for understanding that the educational system is not set up for them to be successful. The educational system in the U.S. poses an opportunity gap for Latinx (and other children

A child telling his story in Spanish while his teacher, Rocío, writes it

of color), not the often cited "achievement gap." Children cannot achieve without the support and tools necessary to be successful; where there is a lack of equity and access, there is a lack of opportunity.

Throughout this book, I have asked you to view Latinx children through an asset-based lens and recognize that they come to school possessing knowledge and skills, which you can build upon in your teaching. For that to happen, you must first "acknowledge that students have significant experiences, insights, and talents to bring to their learning, and second, finding ways to use them in the classroom" (Nieto, 1999). Latinx children's literature is an instrument that can be utilized to uncover the resources Latinx children possess while providing non-Latinx children the windows or sliding glass doors necessary to begin to gain an understanding of our global world. For some children, Latinx literature is a mirror reflecting their language and culture while for others it provides windows and doors to peek into different ways of being in the world.

Praxis

Paulo Freire (1972) defined *praxis* as "reflection and action upon the world in order to transform it." In other words, working to create a more equitable world. For teachers, that means:

Latinx children's literature can serve as the foundation for a curriculum where all students are seen, heard, represented, and included.

- reflecting on and readjusting their teaching to provide all students access to the curriculum;
- examining the curriculum to see where the holes are;
- using students' multiple ways of making meaning as the foundation for teaching and learning;
- integrating aspects of local community and local cultures in the curriculum;
- using student-centered and collaborative instructional strategies;
- utilizing the gift of language that many students bring to school; and finally,
- knowing your students and their families.

Twenty years later, Sonia Nieto (1992) suggested that multicultural literature must saturate the curriculum and offered five functions the literature served:

1. Provide information;
2. Offer differing perspectives, which can change students' views of their world;
3. Encourage or expand an appreciation for diversity;
4. Can lead to critical inquiry; and
5. Bring joy to its readers and "illuminate human experience, in both its unity and variety."

Latinx children's literature can serve as the foundation for a curriculum where all students are seen, heard, represented, and included.

How to Create Change

The Cuban poet and revolutionary, José Martí, said, "Books console us, calm us, prepare us, enrich us and redeem us." As educators, we need to do everything we can to make the power of books accessible to all our students. To engage our students successfully, we should seek out Latinx literature, and also:

Become and Stay Informed

We need to be aware of the issues and concerns and make informed decisions about the literature we use to teach. How do we remain aware? Walk outside of the school and get to know the community. Many of my home visits took place in the community. Talk with community members. I learned a lot by talking with the librarian who also happens to live in the school neighborhood.

Work With Families

Invite your families into the classroom and let them peruse the Latinx literature. If that literature is from their home countries, they can speak to its authenticity—or lack thereof! At the very least, you can engage in conversations and get to know them. Use your families as resources and engage them in your classroom in ways that "respect their strengths and backgrounds rather than patronizing and alienating them, the typical ways families were often treated" (Olivos, Ochoa, & Jiménez-Castellanos, 2011). Ask them to come in and do read-alouds or better yet, tell stories! Do remember that relationships take time; your families are not going to trust you right away. Be patient and work with your families; demonstrate respect for the families and you will get it back.

Do Not Be Afraid to Ask Questions

If you have questions about aspects of the language or culture of your families, ask them. As long as you are respectful and open to getting to know them, they will welcome the questions and likely be more than happy to help you. When I first arrived in Tucson, I did not know what green corn tamales were; my mother made Colombian tamales and that was my knowledge base. While talking with one of the mothers at dismissal one day, I shared this with her—she was horrified! *¿Cómo es eso, nunca ha comido un tamal de elote?* The next time she made them, she sent me a dozen!

If you have questions about aspects of the language or culture of your families, ask them.

Read Latinx Children's Literature

Latinx children's literature is not just for children. There are texts that are so cutting edge and sophisticated that they inform and invigorate adults as well. Flores, Clark, and Smith (2016) suggest that "educators can use it [Latinx lit] to enhance their compassion, heighten their understanding and capacity to deal with controversial issues, increase their knowledge of the lives of Latino students, and augment their capacity to connect with their Latino students." For outsiders to the culture, the books can serve as ambassadors to the culture represented (assuring that the book is accurate and authentic, see Chapter Three).

Celebrate Children's Abilities and Flexibilities With More Than One Language

The message that being bilingual or knowing Spanish is somehow detrimental is heard and internalized by our Latinx children; Latinx children's literature can be used as a tool to recognize and celebrate children's linguistic abilities. Show your students that you value their bilingualism; when reading books with words in Spanish, ask your Latinx students for help with pronunciation. Make sure to do this ahead of time so that children are not put on the spot.

Find Colleagues Who Will Support You

Incorporating Latinx literature into the curriculum is a little easier if you can do it with a colleague. Working with a colleague allows you to exchange ideas and broaden your scope. It is important to make sure that your collaboration does not happen only during Hispanic Heritage Month. We want to make Latinx literature a part of the entire curriculum all year and get away from the food, folklore, fashion, and festivals.

Do All You Can to Ensure School Is About *Nosotros*

Latinx children's literature is not only for Latinx children. That said, it is of utmost importance to the Latinx children in your classroom. Encourage all of your students to be proud of who they are (Latinx and non-Latinx): "The homogenization of U.S. youth ensures the perpetuation of static views of U.S. culture and a resistance toward diversity and a changing America" (Gutiérrez, Baquendano & López, 2000). Latinx children's literature provides students a view into the world as it really is versus what some think it should be.

Concluding Thought

I wrote this book to provide you with a resource for understanding Latinx children's literature and why it is important. Paulo Freire (1972) called on us to be agents of change and work to make the world equitable. As teachers, this encompasses helping children reach their full potential by recognizing and building curricula on the skills and talents they bring to school. Latinx children's literature allows students to tap into the strengths and schema they already bring from home. Be the educator who works to transform teaching and learning and who supports students in reaching their dreams.

References

Ada, A. F. (2016). Foreword: Literature in the lives of Latinx children. In Clark, E. R., Flores, B. B., Smith, H. L., & Gonzalez, D. A. (Eds.). *Multicultural literature for Latinx bilingual children: Their words, their worlds*. Washington, DC: Rowman & Littlefield.

Ada, A. F. (2003). *A magical encounter: Latinx children's literature in the classroom*. Boston, MA: Allyn & Bacon/Longman Publishers.

Ada, A. F., & Zubizarreta, R. (2001). Parent narratives: The cultural bridge between Latino parents and their children. In J. J. Halcon & M. L. Reyes (Eds.), *The best for our children: Critical perspectives on literacy for Latino students* (pp. 229–245). New York: Teachers College Press.

Alvarez, S. (2017). *Community literacies en confianza: Learning from bilingual after-school programs*. Urbana: IL, NCTE.

Anzaldúa, G. (2007). *Borderlands: The new mestiza*. San Francisco, CA: Aunt Lute Books.

Banks, J. A., & Banks, C. A. (1993). Multicultural education. *Phi Delta Kappan, 75*(1), 22–28.

Banks, J. (1988). *Multicultural leader vol 1(2)*

Bartolomé, L. I. (2003). Beyond the methods fetish: Toward a humanizing pedagogy. In A. Darder, M. Baltodano, & R. Torres (Eds.), *The critical pedagogy reader* (pp. 408–429). New York: Routledge Falmer.

Bernal, D. D. (2002). Critical race theory, Latino critical theory, and critical raced-gendered epistemologies: Recognizing students of color as holders and creators of knowledge. *Qualitative inquiry, 8*(1), 105–126.

Bernal, D. D., & Alemán, E., Jr. (2017). *Transforming educational pathways for Chicana/o students: A Critical Race Feminista Practice*. New York: Teachers College Press.

Berzins, M. E., & López, A. E. (2001). Starting off right: Planting the seeds for biliteracy. In M. L. Reyes & J. J. Halcón, (Eds.), *The best for our children; Critical perspectives on literacy for Latino students*. New York: Teachers College Press.

Bishop, R. S. (2003). Reframing the debate about cultural authenticity. *Stories matter: The complexity of cultural authenticity in children's literature*, 25–37.

Bishop, R. S. (1997). Selecting literature for a multicultural curriculum. In V. J. Harris (Ed.), *Using multiethnic literature in the K8 classroom* (pp. 1–20). Norwood, MA: Christopher.

Bishop, R. S. (1992). Multicultural literature for children: Making informed choices. In V. J. Harris (Ed.), *Teaching multicultural literature in grades K–8* (pp. 37–53). Washington, DC: Rowman & Littlefield.

Bishop, R. S. (1990). Mirrors, windows, and sliding glass doors. *Perspectives, 6*(3), ix–xi.

Bradford, C. (2007). *Unsettling narratives: Postcolonial readings of children's literature*. Waterloo, ON, Canada: Wilfrid Laurier University Press.

Botelho, M. J., & Rudman, M. K. (2009). *Critical multicultural analysis of children's literature: Mirrors, windows, and doors*. New York: Routledge.

Bucholz, M., Casillas, D. I., & Lee, J. S. (2017). Language and culture as sustenance. In D. Paris & H. S. Alim (Eds.), *Culturally sustaining pedagogies: Teaching and learning for justice in a changing world*. New York: Teachers College Press.

Campoy, F. I., & Ada, A. F. (2011). Latino literature for children and adolescents. In L. A. Smolen & R. A. Oswald, (Eds.). (2010). *Multicultural Literature and Response: Affirming Diverse Voices: Affirming Diverse Voices*. ABC-CLIO pp. 195–229.

Carger, C. L. (2005). The art of narrative inquiry: Embracing emotion and seeing transformation. In J. Phillion, M. F. He & F. M. Connelly (Eds.), *Narrative & experience in multicultural education* (pp. 231–245). Thousand Oaks, CA: Sage Publications.

Carter, K. (1993). The place of story in the study of teaching and teacher education. *Educational Researcher, 22* (1) 1 (Jan.-Feb. 1993), pp. 5–12. Published by: American Educational Research Association.

Carter, P. L., & Welner, K. G. (Eds.). (2013). *Closing the opportunity gap: What America must do to give every child an even chance*. Northamptonshire, UK: Oxford University Press.

Choo, S. S. (2013). Reading the World, the Globe, and the Cosmos: Approaches to Teaching Literature for the Twenty-First Century. *Global Studies in Education. Volume 28*. New York: Peter Lang Publishing Group.

Clark, E. R., & Flores, B. B. (2016). Preface: *Derrumbando fronteras*/Breaking boundaries. In E. R. Clark, B. B. Flores, H. L. Smith, and D. A. González (Eds.) *Multicultural literature for Latino bilingual children: Their words, their worlds*. Washington, DC: Rowman & Littlefield.

Cummins, J. (2000). Language, power and pedagogy: Bilingual children in the crossfire (Vol. 23). *Multilingual Matters*.

Cummins, J. (2001). Bilingual children's mother tongue: Why is it important for education? *SPROGFORUM, (NR. 19)*, 15–20. Retrieved from http://langpolicy.saschina.wikispaces.net/file/view/CumminsENG.pdf.

Darder, A., & Torres, R. A. (2014). *Latinos and education: A critical reader*. New York: Routledge.

Davila, S., Michaels, C., Hurtado, M., Roldan, M., & Duran-Graybow, I. (2016). Falling Behind: Understanding the Educational Disparities Faced by Immigrant Latino Students in the US. (report) Apr 29, 2016.

DeNicolo, C. P., & Franquiz, M. E. (2006). "Do I have to say it?": Critical Encounters with Multicultural Children's Literature. *Language Arts, 84*(2), 157–170.

DeGuzmán, M. (2017). Latinx: ¡ Estamos aquí! or being "Latinx" at UNC-chapel hill. *Cultural Dynamics, 29*(3), 214–230.

Delgado-Gaitán, C. (2014). Culture, literacy, and power in family-community-school relationships. In A. Darder & R. D. Torres (Eds) *Latinos and Education: A critical reader 2nd edition*. New York: Routledge.

Delgado-Gaitán, C. (2001). *The power of community: Mobilizing for family and schooling*. Washington, DC: Rowman & Littlefield.

Delgado Bernal, D. (2000). Historical struggles for educational equity: Setting the context for Chicano/a schooling today. In C. Tejeda, C. Martinez & Z. Leonardo (Eds.), *Charting new terrains of Chicana(o) /Latina(o) education*. Cresskill, NJ: Hampton Press, Inc.

Edwards, P. (2016). *New ways to engage parents: Strategies and tools for teachers and leaders, K–12.* New York: Teachers College Press.

Espinosa, C. M., & Ascenzi-Moreno, L. (2021) *Rooted in strength: Using Translanguaging to Grow Multilingual Readers and Writers.* New York: Scholastic.

Ferlazzo, L. (2011). What's the difference? Involvement or Engagement? *Schools, Families, Communities* 68(8) pp. 10–14.

Flores, B. B., Clark, E. R., & Smith, H. L. (2016). Latino children's multicultural literature and literacy practices as social imagination: Becoming a culturally efficacious educator. In Clark, E. R., Flores, B. B., Smith, H. L. & González, D. A. (Eds.), *Multicultural literature for Latino bilingual children: Their words, their worlds.* Washington, DC: Rowman & Littlefield.

Fleming, J., Catapano, S, Thompson, C. M., & Carrillo, S. R. (2016). *More mirrors in the classroom: Using urban children's literature to increase literacy.* Washington, DC: Rowman & Littlefield.

Freire, P. (1970). *Pedagogy of the oppressed.* New York: Seabury.

Freire, P., & Macedo, D. (1987). *Literacy: Reading the word and the world.* Westport, CT: Bergin & Garvey.

Freeman, Y. S., & Freeman, D. E. (2002). Closing the achievement gap: How to reach limited-formal-schooling and long-term English learners. *Journal of Adolescent & Adult Literacy, 46*(2), 191.

Gándara, P. (1995). *Over the ivy walls: the educational mobility of low income Chicanos.* New York: SUNY Press.

Gándara, P. (2008). The Crisis in the Education of Latino Students Civil Rights Project/Proyecto Derechos Civiles, University of California–Los Angeles, is a Research Brief from the NEA Research Visiting Scholars Series, Spring 2008, vol. 1a. http://www.nea.org/home/17404.htm

García, O. (2009). *Bilingual Education in the 21st century: A global perspective.* Malden, MA: Wiley-Blackwell.

García. O., Kleifgen, J. O., & Falchi, L. (2008). *From English Language Learners to Emergent Bilinguals Campaign for Educational Equity.* Teachers College, Columbia University.

Gilton, D. (2007). *Multicultural and ethnic children's literature in the United States.* Lanham, MD: Scarecrow Press.

González, N. (2006). *Testimonios* of border identities: "Una mujer acomedida donde quiera cabe". In Delgado Bernal, D., Elenes, C.A., Godínez, F. E., & Villenas, S. (Eds.), *Chicana/Latina Education in everyday life: Feminista perspectives on pedagogy and epistemology.* Albany, New York: SUNY Press.

González, T. (2009). Art, activism, and community: An introduction to Latino/a literature. In M. P. Stewart & Y. Atkinson (Eds.), *Ethnic literary traditions in American children's literature.* New York: Palgrave, McMillon.

González, N., Moll, L. C., & Amanti, C. (Eds.). (2006). *Funds of knowledge: Theorizing practices in households, communities, and classrooms.* New York: Routledge.

González, C., & Gándara, P. (2005). Why we like to call ourselves Latinas. *Journal of Hispanic Higher Education, 4*(4), 392–398.

Gracia, J. E. (2000). *Hispanic/Latino identity: A philosophical perspective.* Malden, MA: Blackwell Publishers, Inc.

Gutiérrez, K., Baquedano-López, P., & Álvarez, H. H. (2000). The crisis in Latino education: The norming of America. In C. Tejeda, C. Martinez & Z. Leonardo, (2000). *Charting New Terrains of Chicana (o)/Latina (o) Education.* pp. 213–232. Cresskill, NJ: Hampton Press.

Guerra, J. C. (1998). *Close to home: Oral and literate practices in a transnational Mexicano community.* New York: Teachers College Press.

Guevara, S. (2003). Authentic enough: Am I? Are you? Interpreting culture for children's literature. In D. L. Fox & K. G. Short (2003). (Eds) *Stories matter: The complexity of cultural authenticity in children's literature.* Urbana, IL: NCTE.

Harris, V. J. (1997). *Using multiethnic literature in the K–8 classroom.* Washington, DC: Rowman & Littlefield.

Harvey, S., Ward, A., & Pilkey, D. (2017). *From striving to thriving: How to grow confident, capable readers.* New York: Scholastic.

Hassett, D. D., & Curwood, J. S. (2009). Theories and practices of multimodal education: The instructional dynamics of picture books and primary classrooms. *The Reading Teacher, 63*(4), 270–282.

Huerta, M. E. S., & Tafolla, C. (2016). En aquel entonces y hoy en día: Using Latino children's Literature to situate social studies education. In Clark, R. E., Flores, B. B., Smith, H. L., & González, D. A. (Eds.). *Multicultural literature for Latino bilingual children: their words, their worlds.*

Johnson, N. J., Koss, M. D., & Martinez, M. (2018). Through the sliding glass door: #EmpowerTheReader. *The Reading Teacher, 71*(5), 569–577.

Johnson, H., Mathis, J., & Short, K. G. (Eds.). (2019). *Critical Content Analysis of Visual Images in Books for Young People: Reading Images.* New York: Routledge.

Kim, H. Y., & Short, K. G. (2019). A picturebook as a cultural artifact: The influence of embedded ideologies. In H. Johnson, J. Mathis & K. G. Short, (Eds.), *Critical content analysis of visual images in books for young people: Reading images.* New York: Routledge.

Krashen, S. (1982). *Principles and practice in second language acquisition.*

López-Robertson, J, (2004). *Making sense of literature through story: Young Latinas using stories as meaning-making devices during literature discussions.* (Unpublished doctoral dissertation.) University of Arizona.

López-Robertson, J. (2010). "Lo agarraron y lo echaron pa'tras": Discussing critical social issues with Young Latinas. *Columbian Applied Linguistics Journal*

López-Robertson, J. (2012). *Language Arts, 90*(1) pp. 30–43

López-Robertson, J. (2014). My gift to you is my language: Spanish is the language of my heart. In B. Kabuto & P. Martens (Eds.), *Linking Families, Learning, and Schooling: Parent–Researcher Perspectives.* New York: Routledge.

López-Robertson, J. (2016). Explorations of identity with Latina mothers. In K. Short, D. Day & J. Schroeder (Eds.), *Teaching Globally: Reading the world through literature.* Portsmouth, NH: Stenhouse.

López-Robertson, J., & Haney, M. J. (2016). Making it happen: Risk-taking and relevance in a rural elementary school. In S. Long, M. Souto-Manning & V. Vasquez, (Eds.), *Courageous leadership in early childhood education: Taking a stand for social justice.* New York: Teachers College Press.

Mann, H. (1848). Twelfth annual report to the Massachusetts Board of Education. *The republic and the school: Horace Mann and the education of free men.*

Mapp, K., Carver, I., & Lander, J. (2017). *Powerful partnerships: A teacher's guide to engaging families for student success.* New York: Scholastic.

Marian, V., & Shook, A. (2012, September). The cognitive benefits of being bilingual. In Cerebrum: The Dana forum on brain science (Vol. 2012). Dana Foundation.

Martínez-Roldán, C. M. (2013). The representation of Latinos and the use of Spanish: A critical content analysis of Skippyjon Jones. *Journal of Children's Literature, 39*(1), 5.

Meyer, C. F., & Rhoades, E. K. (2006) Multiculturalism: Beyond Food, Festival, Folklore, and Fashion, *Kappa Delta Pi Record, 42*:2, 82–87, DOI: 10.1080/00228958.2006.10516439

Morales, Y. (2011). Splendid treasures of mi corazón. In J. C. Naidoo (Ed.), *Celebrating cuentos: Promoting Latino children's literature and literacy in classrooms and libraries.* Santa Barbara, CA: Libraries Unlimited.

Naidoo, J. C., & López-Robertson, J. (2007). Descubriendo el sabor: Spanish bilingual book publishing and cultural authenticity. *Multicultural Review, 16*(4), 24.

National Center for Education Statistics, *Back to school by the numbers 2019-2020.* https://nces.ed.gov/programs/digest/d19/tables/dt19_203.60.asp. Retrieved March 18, 2021.

National Center for Education Statistics, https://nces.ed.gov/programs/coe/indicator_cgf.asp. Retrieved March 12, 2021.

National Council of Teachers of English https://ncte.org/statement/ipoc/

Nieto, S. (2010). *The light in their eyes: Creating multicultural learning communities.* New York: Teachers College Press.

Nieto, S. (2001). Foreword. In M. L. Reyes & J. J. Halcón, (Eds.), *The best for our children: Critical perspectives on literacy for Latino students.* New York: Teachers College Press.

Nieto, S. (1999). *The light in their eyes: Creating multicultural learning communities.* New York: Teachers College Press.

Nieto, S. (1997). We have stories to tell: Puerto Ricans in children's literature. In V. J. Harris (Ed.). *Using multiethnic literature in the K–8 classroom.* Washington, DC: Rowman & Littlefield.

Nieto, S. (1992). *Affirming diversity: The sociopolitical context of multicultural education.* New York: Longman.

Noddings, N. (1991). Stories in dialogue: Caring and interpersonal reasoning. In C. Witherell & N. Noddings (Eds.), *Stories lives tell: Narrative and dialogue in education* (pp. 157–170). New York: Teachers College Press.

Olivos, E. M., Ochoa, A. M., & Jiménez-Castellanos, O. (2011). Critical voices in bicultural parent involvement: A framework for transformation. In E. M. Olivos, O. Jiménez-Castellanos & A. M. Ochoa (Eds.), *Bicultural parent engagement: Advocacy and empowerment* (pp. 1–20). New York: Teachers College Press.

Ostrom, H. (2003). Story, stories, and you. In W. Bishop & H. Ostrom (Eds.), The subject is story: Essays for writers and readers (pp. 2–9). Portsmouth, NH: Heinemann.

Paley, V. G. (1990). *The boy who would be a helicopter: The uses of storytelling in the classroom.* Cambridge, MA: Harvard University.

Pew Hispanic Center (2020). *About One-in-Four U.S. Hispanics Have Heard of Latinx, but Just 3% Use It.* Retrieved March 11, 2021 from https://www.pewresearch.org/hispanic/2020/08/11/about-one-in-four-u-s-hispanics-have-heard-of-latinx-but-just-3-use-it

Pew Hispanic Center (2020). *Pew Hispanic Center Fact Tank.* https://www.pewresearch.org/fact-tank/2020/09/10/key-facts-about-u-s-latinos-for-national-hispanic-heritage-month

Pew Hispanic Center (2019). *Pew Hispanic Center Fact Sheet.* Retrieved January 10, 2020, from https://www.pewresearch.org/hispanic/fact-sheet/u-s-hispanics-facts-on-mexican-origin-latinos

Pew Hispanic Center (2019). *Pew Hispanic Center Key Facts about Hispanics.* Retrieved January 10, 2020 from https://www.pewresearch.org/fact-tank/2019/09/16/key-facts-about-u-s-hispanics

Pew Hispanic Center (2017). *Pew Hispanic Center Statistical Portrait of Hispanics in the U.S.* Retrieved January 10, 2020, from https://www.pewresearch.org/hispanic/2017/09/18/2015-statistical-information-on-hispanics-in-united-states/#share-mexican-origin

Ray, K. W., & Cleveland, L. B. (2004). About the Authors: Writing Workshop With Our Youngest Writers. *Education Review.*

Salinas Jr., C. (2020). The complexity of the "x" in Latinx: How Latinx/a/o students relate to, identify with and understand the term Latinx. *Journal of Hispanic Higher Education, 19*(2), 149–168.

Salinas Jr., C., & Lozano, A. (2019). Mapping and recontextualizing the evolution of the term Latinx: An environmental scanning in higher education. *Journal of Latinos and Education, 18*(4), 302–315.

Sánchez, P., & Landa, M. (2016). Cruzando fronteras: Negotiating the stories of Latino immigrant and transnational children. In Clark, E. R., Flores, B. B., Smith, H. L., & Gonzalez, D. A. (Eds.). *Multicultural literature for Latinx bilingual children: Their words, their worlds.* Washington, DC: Rowman & Littlefield.

Scott, J. C., Straker, D. Y., & Katz, L., (2009). Cross-currents in language policies and pedagogical practices. In J. C. Scott, D. Y. Straker & L. Katz, (Eds.), *Affirming students' right to their own language: Bridging language policies and pedagogies.* New York: NCTE/Routledge.

Schon, I. (2004). *Recommended Books in Spanish for Children and Young Adults: 2000 through 2004.* Scarecrow Press.

Serrato, P. (2009). Conflicting inclinations: Luis J. Rodríguez's picture books for children. In M. P. Stewart & Y. Atkinson (Eds.), *Ethnic literary traditions in American children's literature.* New York: Palgrave, McMillon.

Shor, I. (1992). *Empowering Education: Critical teaching for social change.* The University of Chicago Press.

Shor, I. (1999). What is critical literacy? *Journal for pedagogy, pluralism, and Practice vol 1*(4) article 2. Available at https://digitalcommons.lesley.edu/jppp/vol1/iss4/2

Short, K. G. (2016). A curriculum that is intercultural. In K. G. Short, D. Day & J. Schroeder (Eds.), *Teaching globally: Reading the world through literature* (pp. 3–24). Portland, ME: Stenhouse.

Short, K., & Fox, D. (2003). About the cover. In D. L. Fox & K. G. Short (2003). (Eds.). *Stories matter: The complexity of cultural authenticity in children's literature*. Urbana, IL: NCTE. pp.v.

Smolen, L. A., & Oswald, R. A. (Eds.). (2011). *Multicultural Literature and Response: Affirming Diverse Voices: Affirming Diverse Voices*. ABC-CLIO.

Spooner, M. (2003). The stories we are: Old Meshikee and the winter of 1929. In W. Bishop & H. Ostrom (Eds.), *The subject is story: Essays for writers and readers* (pp. 51–61). Portsmouth, NH: Heinemann.

Springer, P., Hollist, C., & Buchfink, K. (2009). Engaging Latinxs in culturally specific educational programming: A multidisciplinary approach. *Family and Consumer Sciences Research Journal, 37*(3), pp. 310–328.

United States Census Bureau (2019). *America counts: Stories behind the numbers*. Retrieved October 10, 2020 from https://www.census.gov/library/stories/2019/02/hispanic-poverty-rate-hit-an-all-time-low-in-2017.html

Walker, A., Shafer, J., & Iiams, M. (2004). Not in my classroom": Teacher attitudes towards English language learners in the mainstream classroom. *NABE Journal of Research and Practice, 2*(1), 130–160.

Valdés, G. (1996). *Con respeto: Bridging the distance between culturally diverse families and schools*. New York: Teachers College Press.

Valenzuela, A. (1999). *Subtractive Schooling: US Mexican Youth and the Politics of Caring*. New York: State University of New York Press.

Vardell, S., & Wong, J. (2015). *The poetry Friday anthology for celebrations: Holiday poems* for the whole year in Spanish and English. Pomelo Books.

Vasquez, V. M., Tate, S. L., & Harste, J. C. (2013). *Negotiating critical literacies with teachers: Theoretical foundations and pedagogical resources for pre-service and In-service contexts*. New York: Routledge.

Vogel, S. & García, O. (2017, December 19). Translanguaging. *Oxford Research Encyclopedia of Education*. Retrieved 24 Jan 2021 from https://oxfordre.com/education/view/10.1093/acrefore/9780190264093.001.0001/acrefore-9780190264093-e-181

Worlds of Words: Center of Global Literacies and Literature at the University of Arizona. (2020). *10 quick ways to analyze children's books for racism and sexism*. Retrieved October 10, 2020 from http://wowlit.org/links/evaluating-global-literature/10-quick-ways-to-analyze-childrens-books-for-racism-and-sexism

Children's Literature Cited

The page numbers following each entry note the page where the book is referenced.

Ada, A. F. (2001). *Gathering the Sun: An Alphabet in Spanish and English*. S. Silva (Illus.). HarperCollins. (p. 38)

Ada, A. F. (1995). *My Name Is Maria Isabel* (K. D. Thompson, Illus.). Atheneum Books for Young Readers. (pp. 83, 98)

Ada, A. F., & Campoy, I. (2013). *Yes! We Are Latinos: Poems and Prose About the Latino Experience* (D. Diaz, Illus.). Charlesbridge. (p. 95)

Ada, A. F., & Campoy, F. Isabel & Schertle, A. (2006). *Pio Peep! Traditional Spanish Nursery Rhymes Book and CD* (V. Escriva, Illus.). HarperCollins Español. (p. 92)

Alarcón, F. X. (2005). *Angels Ride Bikes and Other Fall Poems: Los ángeles andan en bicicleta: Y otros poemas de otoño* (M. C. González, Illus.). Children's Book Press. (p. 96)

Altman, L. J. (1995). *El camino de Amelia* (E. O. Sánchez, Illus.), Lee & Low Books. (pp. 92, 111–112)

Anaya, R. (1972). *Bless Me, Ultima*. Quinto Sol. (p. 37)

De Anda, D. (2019). *Mango Moon: When Deportation Divides a Family* (S. Cornelison, Illus.). Albert Whitman & Company. (p. 100)

Andrews-Goebe, N., (2011). *The Pot That Juan Built* (D. Diaz, Illus.). Lee & Low Books. (p. 92)

Anzaldúa, G (1997). *Friends From the Other Side/Amigos del otro lado* (C. Méndez, Illus.). Children's Book Press. (p. 100)

Argueta, J. (2017). *Salsa* (D. Tonatiuh, Illus.) Groundwood Books. (p. 95)

Argueta, J. (2016). *Guacamole: Un poema para cocinar/A Cooking Poem* (M. Sada, Illus.). Groundwood Books. (p. 95)

Argueta, J. (2008). *Xóchitl and the Flowers/Xóchitl, la niña de las flores* (C. Angel, Illus.). Children's Book Press. (p. 93)

Argueta, J. (2008). *A Movie in My Pillow/Una película en mi almohada* (E. Gómez, Illus.). Children's Book Press. (p. 96)

Argueta, J. (2006). *Talking with Mother Earth/Hablando con Madre Tierra: Poems/Poemas* (L. A. Perez, Illus.). Groundwood Books. (p. 96)

Arnold, M. D. (2019). *Galápagos Girl/Galapagueña* (A. Domínguez, Illus.). Lee & Low Books. (p. 94)

Beaty, A. (2019). *Sofia Valdez, Future Prez* (D. Roberts, Illus.). Harry N. Abrams. (p. 94)

Belpré, P. (1932). *Pérez and Martina: A Portorican Folk Tale*. Frederick Warne & Co. (p. 39)

Belpré, P. (1965). *The Tiger and the Rabbit and Other Tales* (T. De Paola, Illus.). J. B. Lippincott Company. (p. 39)

Bertrand, D. G. (2015). *The Empanadas that Abuela Made/Las empanadas que hacía la abuela* (A. P. DeLange, Illus.) Arte Público Press. (p.77)

Bowles, D. (2018). *They Call Me Güero: A Border Kid's Poems* (D. Bowles, Illus.). Cinco Puntos Press. (pp. 84, 101)

Brown, M. (2017). *Frida Kahlo and Her Animalitos* (J. Parra, Illus.). North South Books. (p. 90)

Brown, M. (2010). *Side by Side/Lado a Lado: The Story of Dolores Huerta and César Chávez/La historia de Dolores Huerta y César Chávez* (J. Cepeda, Illus.). HarperCollins Español. (p. 98)

Brown, M. (2005). *My name Is/Me llamo Gabriela: The life of/La vida de Gabriela Mistral Who Became the First Nobel Prize-winning Latina Woman in the World*. (J. Parra, Illus.). Cooper Square Publishing LLC. (p. 90)

Buitrago, J. (2015). *Two White Rabbits* (R. Yockteng, Illus.). Groundwood Books. (p. 99)

Campoy, F. I., & Howell, T. (2016). *Maybe Something Beautiful: How Art Transformed a Neighborhood* (R. López, Illus.). HMH Books for Young Readers. (p. 94)

Cofer, J. O. (2005). *¡A bailar!/Let's Dance!* (C. A. Rodríguez, Illus.). Piñata Books. (p. 72)

Cohn, D. (2005). *¡Si, se puede!/Yes, We Can!: Janitor Strike in L.A.* (F. Delgado, Illus.). Cinco Puntos Press. (p. 97)

Costales, A. (2007). *Abuelita Full of Life: Abuelita llena de vida* (M. Aviles, Illus.). Cooper Square Publishers, LLC. (p. 92)

Da Coll, I. (2005). *Azúcar* (I. Da Coll, Illus.). Lectorum Publications. (p. 13)

Delacre, L. (1992). *Arroz con leche: canciones y ritmos populares de América Latina/Popular Songs and Rhymes From Latin America* (L. Delacre, Illus.). Scholastic. (p. 92)

Denise, A. A. (2019). *Planting Stories: The Life of Librarian and Storyteller Pura Belpré* (P. Escobar, Illus.). HarperCollins. (p. 39)

Díaz, J. (2018) *Islandborn* (L. Espinosa, Illus.). Dial Books. (p. 21)

Dominguez, A. (2019). *Stella Díaz Has Something to Say* (A. Dominguez, Illus.). Square Fish. (p. 27)

Dominguez, A. (2021). *Stella Díaz Never Gives Up* (A. Dominguez, Illus.). Roaring Books Press. (p. 94)

Domínguez, G. H. (2019). *Dear Abuelo* (T. Martínez, Illus.). Reycraft Books. (pp. 91, 99)

Dorros, A. (2014). *Papá and Me* (Gutierrez, Illus.). HarperCollins. (p. 72)

Dorros, A. (1997). *Radio Man: A Story in English and Spanish* (A. Dorros, Illus.). HarperCollins Español. (p. 100)

Elya, S. M. (2016). *La Madre Goose: Nursery Rhymes for los Niños* (2016). (J. Martínez- Neal, Illus.). G. P. Putnam's Sons Books for Young Readers. (p. 92)

Engle, M. (2021). *A Song of Frutas* (S. Palacios, Illus.). Atheneum Books for Young Readers. (pp. 84, 92)

Engle, M. (2017). *All the Way to Havana* (M. Curato, Illus.). Henry Holt & Co. (pp. 21, 84)

Engle, M. (2015). *Drum Dream Girl: How One Girl's Courage Changed Music* (R. López, Illus.). HMH Books for Young Readers (pp. 84, 94)

Garza, C. L. (2017). *Lucía la Luchadora* (A. Bermúdez, Illus.). POW! Kids Books. (pp. 88, 89)

Garza, C. L. (2018). *Lucía la Luchadora and the Million Masks* (A. Bermúdez, Illus.). POW! Kids Books. (p. 89)

Garza, C. L. (1990). *Family Pictures/Cuadros de familia*. Children's Book Press. (p. 39)

Garza, J. (2007). *Lucha Libre: The Man in the Silver Mask: A Bilingual Cuento* (X. Garza, Illus.). Cinco Puntos Press. (pp. 87, 88)

González, M. (2013). *My Colors, My World/Mis colores, mi mundo* (M. González, Illus.). Lee & Low Books. (p. 81–82, 84, 86)

González, M. (2014). *Call Me Tree/Llámame arbol* (M. González, Illus.). Children's Book Press. (p. 81)

González, M. C. (2009). *I know the river loves me* (M. González, Illus.). Children's Book Press. (pp. 70, 81–82, 84)

González. R. (2016). *Antonio's Card/La tarjeta de Antonio* (C. Álvarez, Illus.). Lee & Low Books. (p. 41)

González. R. (2014). *Soledad Sigh-Sighs/Soledad suspiros* (R. Ibarra, Illus.). Children's Book Press. (p. 41)

González, S., & Brown, M. (2018). *Sarai and the Meaning of Awesome*. (C. Almeda, Illus.). Scholastic. (pp. 41, 83)

Grande, R. (2016). *The Distance Between Us: Young Readers Edition*. Aladdin. (p. 101)

Griego, M, Bucks, B., Gilbert, S., & Kimball, L. (1988) *Tortillitas para Mamá and Other Nursery Rhymes* (B. Cooney, Illus.). Square Fish. (p. 92)

Hale, C. (2019). *All Equal: A Ballad of Lemon Grove/Todos iguales: Un corrido de Lemon Grove* (C. Hale, Illus.). Lee & Low Books. (pp. 23, 97)

Herrera, J. F. (2018). *Imagine* (L. Castillo, Illus.). Candlewick. (p. 95)

Herrera, J. F. (2006). *The Upside Down Boy/El niño de cabeza* (E. Gomez, Illus.) Children's Book Press. (p. 85)

Herrera, J. F. (2003). *Super Cilantro Girl/La Superniña del Cilantro* (H. R. Tapia, Illus.). Children's Book Press. (p. 85)

Herrera, J. F. (2001). *Calling the Doves/El canto de las palomas* (E. Simmons, Illus.). Children's Book Press. (p. 118)

Jiménez, J. (2000). *La mariposa* (S. Silva, Illus.). HMH Books for Young Readers. (p. 112)

Jiménez, J. (1997). *The Circuit: Stories from the Life of a Migrant Child*. University of New Mexico Press (p. 101)

Kunkel, A. B. (2020). *Digging for Words: José Alberto Gutiérrez and the Library He Built* (P. Escobar (Illus.). Schwartz & Wade. (p. 21)

Lachtman, O. D. (1995). *Pepita Talks Twice/Pepita habla dos veces* (A. P. De Lange, Illus.). Arte Público Press. (pp. 42, 125)

Laínez, R. C. (2019). *My Shoes and I: Crossing Three Borders/Mis zapatos y yo: Cruzando tres fronteras.* (F. V. Broeck, Illus.). Arte Público Press. (pp. 85, 99)

Laínez, R. C. (20195). *¡Vámonos! Let's Go!* (J. Cepeda, Illus.). Holiday House. (p. 93)

Laínez, R. C. (2010). *The Tooth Fairy Meets El Raton Perez* (T. Lintern, Illus.). Tricycle Press. (p. 72)

Laínez, R. C. (2009). *René Has Two Last Names/René tiene dos apellidos* (F. G. Ramirez, Illust.). Arte Público Press. (p. 98)

Laínez, R. C. (2006). *Playing Lotería/El juego de la lotería* (J. Arena, Illus.). Cooper Square Publishing LLC. (pp. 92, 124)

Marshall, L. E. (2016). *Rainbow Weaver/Tejedora del arcoíris* (E. Chavarri, Illus.). Children's Book Press. (p. 21)

Martí, J. (1997). *Los zapáticos de rosa.* (L. Delacre, Illus.), Lectorum. (p. 36)

Martínez-Neal, J. (2021). *Zonia's Rain Forest* (J. Martínez-Neal, Illus.). Candlewick. (pp. 85, 93)

Martínez-Neal, J. (201). *Alma and How She Got Her Name* (J. Martínez-Neal, Illus.). Candlewick. (pp. 85, 98)

Mateo, J. M. (2014). *Migrant: The Journey of a Mexican Worker* (J. M. Pedro, Illus.). Harry N. Abrams. (p. 101)

McClure, W. (2021). *A Garden to Save the Birds* (B. Mayumi, Illus.). Albert Whitman & Company. (p. 93)

Medina, M. (2020). *Evelyn Del Rey Is Moving Away* (S. Sanchez, Illus.). Candlewick. (pp. 74–75, 85)

Medina, M. (2017). *Mango, Abuela, and Me* (A. Dominguez, Illus.). Candlewick. (pp. 85, 91)

Méndez, Y. (2019). *Where Are You From?* (J. Kim, Illus.). HarperCollins. (p. 91)

Menéndez, J. (2021) *Latinitas: Celebrating 40 Big Dreamers* (J. Menéndez, Illus.). Henry Holt & Co. (BYR). (p. 89)

Mills, D. (2018). *La frontera: El viaje con papá, My journey With Papa* (C. Navarro, Illus.). Barefoot Books. (p. 99)

Mohr, N. (1993). *El Bronx Remembered*. HarperTeen. (p. 37)

Mora, P. (2018). *Bookjoy Wordjoy* (R. Colón, Illus.). Lee & Low Books. (pp. 86, 96)

Mora, P. (2007) *Yum! ¡MmMm! ¡Qué Rico! America's Sproutings* (R. López, Illus.). Lee & Low Books. (pp. 86, 96)

Mora, P. (2001). *Listen to the Desert/ Oye Al Desierto* (F. X. Mora, Illus.). Clarion Books. (pp. 76–77)

Mora, P. (2000). *Tomás and the Library Lady* (R. Colón, Illus.). Dragonfly Books. (pp. 39, 54, 100, 108–109)

Mora, P. (1999). *Confetti: Poems for Children* (E. O. Sánchez, Illus.). Lee & Low Books. (p. 38)

Mora, P. (1997). *A Birthday Basket for Tía*. Aladdin Picture Books. (p. 38)

Morales, Y. (2018). *Rudas: Niño's Horrendous Hermanitas* (Y. Morales, Illus.). Square Fish (p. 88)

Morales, Y. (2018). *Dreamers* (Y. Morales, Illus.). Neal Porter Books. (pp. 86, 100)

Morales, Y. (2018). *Just in Case: A Trickster Tale and Spanish Alphabet Book* (Y. Morales, Illus.). Square Fish. (p. 86)

Morales, Y. (2016). *Just a Minute: A Trickster Tale and Counting Book* (Y. Morales, Illus.). Chronicle Books. (p. 86)

Morales, Y. (2015). *Niño Wrestles the World* (Y. Morales, Illus.). Square Fish. (pp. 48–49, 51, 76, 86, 87, 88)

Morales, Y. (2014). *Viva Frida* (T. O'Meara, Photographer). Roaring Books Press. (pp. 86, 90)

Mosca, J. F. (2019). *The Astronaut With a Song for the Stars: The Story of Dr. Ellen Ochoa* (D. Rieley, Illus.). The Innovative Press. (p. 90)

Orozco, J. L. (2020). *Sing with Me/ Canta Conmigo: Six Classic Songs in English and Spanish* (S. Palacios, Illus.). Scholastic. (p. 93)

Orozco, J. L. (2005). *Rin, Rin, Rin/Do, Re, Mi* (D. Díaz, Illus.). Scholastic. (pp. 86, 93)

Orozco, J. L. (2002). *Diez Deditos/Ten Little Fingers & Other Play Rhymes and Action Songs from Latin America* (E. Kleven, Illus.). Puffin Books. (pp. 49, 93)

Orozco, J. L. (1999). *De Colores and Other Latin American Folksongs for Children*. NY: Puffin Books. (p. 39, 49, 70, 86)

Otheguy, E., Domínguez, A., & Vidal, B. (2017). *Martí's Song for Freedom/ Martí y sus versos por la libertad*. Lee & Low Books. (p. 98)

de la Peña, M. (2018). *Carmela Full of Wishes* (C. Robinson, Illus.). G. P. Putnam's Sons Books for Young Readers. (p. 72)

Pérez, N. (2021). *Coquí in the City* (N. Pérez, Illus.). Dial Books. (p. 21)

Perkins, M. (2019). *Between Us and Abuela: A Family Story from the Border* (S. Palacios, Illus.). Farrar, Straus and Giroux. (p. 99)

Quintero, I. (2019). *My Papí Has a Motorcycle* (Z. Peña, Illus.). Kokila. (p. 21)

Raúl the Third (2020). *¡Vamos! Let's Go Eat!* (R. Third, Illus.). Versify. (p. 73)

Raúl the Third (2019). *¡Vamos! Let's Go to the Market!* (R. Third, Illus.). Versify. (pp. 73, 89)

Reynoso, N. (2020). *Be Bold! Be Brave! 11 American Latinas who made U.S. History/¡Sé audaz, sé valiente!: 11 latinas que hicieron historia en los Estados Unidos* (J. Leal, Illus.). Con Todo Press. (p. 89)

Rhomer, H., & Gomez, C. (1989). *Mr. Sugar Came to Town/La visita del Sr. Azúcar*. (E. Chagoya, Illus.). San Francisco, CA: Children's Book Press. (pp. 10–14, 39)

Roth, S. L., & Trumbore, C. (2013) *Parrots over Puerto Rico*. Lee & Low Books. (p. 104)

Schachner, J. (2005). *Skippyjon Jones*. (J. Schachner, Illus.). Puffin Books. (p. 55)

Shahan, S. (2007). *Spicy, Hot, Colors/ Colores Picantes* (P. Barrágan, Illus.). August House. (p. 96)

Soto, G. (1996). *Too Many Tamales* (E. Martínez, Illus.). Puffin Books. (p. 38)

Soto, G. (2000). *Baseball in April and other stories*. NY: HMH Books for Young Readers. (p. 38)

Sotomayor, S. (2019). *Just Ask! Be Different, Be Brave, Be You* (R. López, Illus.). Philomel Books. (p. 90)

Sotomayor, S. (2018). *Turning Pages: My Life Story* (L. Delacre, Illus.). Philomel Books. (p. 90)

Tafolla, C. (2009). *What Can You Do with a Paleta?* (M. Morales, Illus.). Tricycle Press. (p. 72)

Tafolla, C. (2009). *What Can You Do With a Rebozo?/¿Qué puedes hacer con un rebozo?* (A. Cordova, Illus.). Tricycle Press. (p. 72)

Tonatiuh, D. (2019). *Soldier for Equality: José de la Luz Sáenz and the Great War* (D. Tonatiuh, Illus.). Harry N. Abrams. (p. 97)

Tonatiuh, D. (2018). *Undocumented: A Worker's Fight* (D. Tonatiuh, Illus.). Harry N. Abrams. (p. 97)

Tonatiuh, D. (2017). *Danza!: Amalia Hernández and El Ballet Folklórico de México* (D. Tonatiuh, Illus.). Abrams Books for Young Readers. (p. 90)

Tonatiuh, D. (2014). *Separate Is Never Equal: Sylvia Mendez and Her Family's Fight for Desegregation* (D. Tonatiuh, Illus.). Harry N. Abrams. (pp. 23, 97, 104)

Tonatiuh, D. (2013). *Pancho Rabbit and the Coyote: A Migrant's Tale* (D. Tonatiuh, Illus.). Harry N. Abrams. (pp. 86, 99)

Tonatiuh, D. (2010). *Dear Primo: A Letter to My Cousin* (D. Tonatiuh, Illus.). Harry N. Abrams. (pp. 73, 86)

The Rise-Home Stories Project & Hernández-Linares, L., (2021). *Alejandria Fights Back/La Lucha de Alejandria*. (R. Liu-Trujillo, Illus.). The Feminist Press at CUNY. (p. 94)

Vamos, S. R. (2019). *The Piñata That the Farm Maiden Hung* (S. Serra, Illus.). Charlesbridge. (p. 92)

Vamos, S. R. (2013). *The Cazuela That the Farm Maiden Stirred* (R. López, Illus.). Charlesbridge. (p. 92)

Velásquez, E. (2021). *Octopus Stew* (E. Velasquez, Illus.). Holiday House. (p. 91)

Velásquez, E. (2013). *Grandma's Gift* (E. Velasquez, Illus.). Bloomsbury USA Childrens. (p. 91)

Velásquez, E. (2004). *Grandma's Records* (E. Velásquez, Illus.). Bloomsbury USA Childrens. (p. 91)

Verde, S. (2018). *Hey, Wall: A Story of Art and Community* (J. Parra, Illus.). Simon & Schuster/Paula Wiseman Books. (p. 94)

Warren, S. (2012). *Dolores Huerta: A Hero to Migrant Workers* (R. Casilla, Illus.). Two Lions. (p. TK)

Weill, C. (2014). *ABeCedarios: Mexican Folk Art ABCs in English and Spanish*. Cinco Puntos Press. (pp. 32, 34)

Winter, J. (2009). *Sonia Sotomayor: A Judge Grows in the Bronx/La juez que creció en el Bronx* (E. Rodríguez, Illus.). Atheneum Books for Young Readers. (p. 90)

Index

A

abuelos/grandparents, text set about, 91–92
accuracy of details, questions for analyzing, 59
acquiring language vs. learning language, 28
Ada, Alma Flor, 15, 34, 116
    profile of, 83
adivinanzas (riddles), 35
advocates, families as, 127–128
asset-based lens, vs. deficit-based, 26, 29, 128, 133
assimilation, 116–117
    vs. multiculturalism, 24
authenticity, cultural, analyzing, 57–60
author, biases of, 66–67
author studies, 81–82
authorship, 57–59
awareness, 132–133

B

believability, questions for analyzing, 59
Belpré, Pura, 38–39
big book, class-made, 10
bilingual abilities, 42
bilingual books, considerations for selecting, 62
bilingualism, 28, 70–71, 70–71126, 135
Bishop, Rudine Sims, 33, 57
book awards, for Latinx literature, 38–39
    book talks, 101–102
    for pláticas literarias, 105
books, bias in, 64–68
Bowles, David, profile of, 84
Brown v. Board of Education, 97, 104
Brown, Monica, profile of, 83

C

Carver, Ilene, 119
Census Bureau, terminology used by, 18
characters, roles of, as indicators of bias, 64
characters, multidimensionality of, as criterion for selecting literature, 61
Chávez, César, 98
Children's Books as a Radical Act movement, 45
children's books by and about colored people, data on, 45, 58
Civil Rights era, 37
class books, bilingual and multicultural, 78–79
classroom library, power of, 80

cliffhangers, during read-alouds, 74
colors white and black, images of, and child's self-image, 66
communicating with families, 119–124
community, connecting with, 134
confianza, 51
connections for readers, questions for analyzing, 60
connections to story, from pláticas literarias, 106–107
Cooperative Children's Book Center (CCBC), 44–45
countries of origin of Latinx people (map), 19
critical pedagogy and critical literacy, 53–54
critical thinking, in pláticas literarias, 106–107
cuentos, shared in pláticas, 104
culture, representation of, as criterion for selecting literature, 61
curriculum, enhanced with Latinx literature, 14–15, 103–104, 133–134

D

Deedy, Carmen Agra, profile of, 84
deep meaning, 54
difference, kids making a, text set about, 93–94
discussions, authentic, 104
drawing, as form of writing, 107–108

E

education, valued by Latinx families, 115–116
education levels, characters', as criterion for selecting literature, 62
empathy, fostered by Latinx literature, 43
Engle, Margarita, profile of, 84
English, as language of power, 116–117
English immersion programs, 24, 28
English language learners (ELLs), 26, 27
"English Only" movement, 25
English, characters' knowledge of, as criterion for selecting literature, 61
esperanza, 7–8, 15
expectations for children, 27, 116, 124
    family's, 116
expressive reading, modeled in read-alouds, 74

ethnicity of authors and audience in books published, data about, 45, 58

F

families, beliefs about, 119–122
family book, 82
family engagement, 105–106, 114–128, 134–135
    in author studies, 81–82
family, depictions of, 63
field trips, writing about, 78
fingerplays, 70, 124
fluency, modeled in read-alouds, 74
folktales, 35
Freire, Paulo, 29, 41, 53, 133–134. 136
Frierson, Tammy, 13, 15, 48, 70, 76
funds of knowledge, 30, 41–42, 116–117, 121–122

G

Gandhi, Mahatma, 132
gender inclusivity, 19
gendered language, 67
González, Maya Christina, 17, 81–82, 102
    profile of, 84

H

heritage language, 42
heroes, bias in, 66
Herrera, Juan Felipe, profile of, 85
Herron, María del Rocío, 13, 35, 77, 119–120, 124
heterogeneity of Latinx community, 44–45, 131
high-poverty schools, 26
Hispanic, 18
Hispanic Heritage Month, 128, 136
home, depictions of, 63
home language, importance of, 71
home visits, 11–12, 52, 123–124
homework, mothers doing, 125
Huerta, Dolores, 90

I

identity, self and ethnic, through Latinx literature, 40–41
illustrations, assessing, 63–64
illustrator studies, 82–83
immigration, text set about, 99–101
inequities faced by Latinx people, 25–26
institutional racism, 114
interactive read-alouds, 74–75
Intercultural Training and Resource Center (ITRC), 9
invisibility, Latinx, in classroom, 17–18

J

justice and equity, text set about, 97–98